SERVICE-ORIENTED SUPPLY CHAIN OPERATIONS

SERVICE-ORIENTED SUPPLY CHAIN OPERATIONS

Song Hua

GALE

Farmington Hills, Mich • Andover, UK • Chicago • Mason, Ohio • Meriden, Conn • New York
San Francisco • Singapore • Waterville, Maine

GALE

Service-Oriented Supply Chain Operations
Song Hua

Publishing Director:
Roy Lee

Editorial Manager:
Yang Liping

Development Editor (Media):
Tanmayee Bhatwadekar

Associate Development Editor:
Doris Wai

Senior Regional Director:
Janet Lim

Product Manager:
Tan Lee Hong

Production Manager:
Pauline Lim

Production Executive:
Cindy Chai

Translator:
Francesca Lim

Copy Editor:
Mahtab Dubash

Cover Designer:
Ong Lay Keng

Compositor:
diacriTech, Inc.

ISBN: 978-981-4410-97-7

Cengage Learning Asia Pte Ltd
30A Kallang Place #12-06
Singapore 339213

Cengage Learning is a leading provider of customized learning solutions with office locations around the globe, including Singapore, the United Kingdom, Australia, Mexico, Brazil and Japan. Locate your local office at **www.cengage.com/global**

To learn more about Gale product information, visit **www.gale.com**

Printed in Singapore
Print Number: 03 Print Year: 2022

Contents

Foreword

Over the past few decades, the tertiary industry has replaced the primary and secondary industries to become the major pillar of wealth creation for many advanced economies. Today, the development of the service industry is often viewed as one of the major indicators to gauge the socioeconomic developments in an economy. China's service industry, which accounts for a 41% share of the gross domestic product (GDP), is lagging behind many economies. The service industry in developed economies typically accounts for a 70% share of the GDP; in metropolises such as New York, London, and Hong Kong, the service industry accounts for 90% of the GDP. The share of the service industry as a percentage of the GDP in China is even lower than the average share of service industry in low-income countries (43%). Against this backdrop, boosting the growth in the service industry is high on the Chinese government's agenda. In the 12th Five-Year Plan, China intends to speed up the development of the service industry, and it is hoped that the contribution of the service industry to China's total GDP will exceed 50% by 2015.

An increasing number of people are realizing the importance of the service industry. In the 1960s, some people held a pessimistic view toward the developments in the service industry. The well-known "Baumol's cost disease," named after the economist William J. Baumol, suggested that it is harder for the labor-intensive service industry than for the goods-producing industry to achieve productivity growth. However, over the years, Baumol's cost disease did not materialize. This is because as the service industry evolves, it becomes more dependent on inputs from sectors such as technology, knowledge, and human capital. The New Growth Theory put forward by Paul Robert in the 1980s suggests that technology and knowledge are significant contributors to economic growth. As compared to the traditional service industry which is labour-intensive, the modern service industry is knowledge-based; it creates higher added value, demonstrates faster growth, and yields better profitability.

Over the past years, we have witnessed tremendous growth in knowledge-based modern service industry sectors such as legal services, management services, engineering services, financial services, and computer services.

In developed economies, modern services are the fastest-growing industry sectors. According to statistics, knowledge-based service sectors have helped create nearly 50% of the job opportunities in the service industry in the European Union. In the United States, the knowledge-based service industry contributes to 50% of the country's GDP. In comparison, the knowledge-based service industry contributes 22.1% of the GDP in South Korea. Today, traditional service sectors such as retail, wholesale, transportation, and catering occupy approximately 40% of the service industry share in China. The knowledge-based service sector in China has huge room for growth.

Today, producer services such as telecommunications, finance, insurance, logistics, and professional consulting occupy a bigger slice of the service industry, accounting for more than half of the industry share in developed economies. The rise of services has brought important changes to the manufacturing sector. "Servitization of manufacturing" is another prominent trend. It has been observed that since the late 20th century, more and more manufacturing enterprises are shifting from selling products to selling integrated products and services that deliver value; services are viewed as a key differentiator for companies to win customers. Services have become an increasingly important revenue and profit contributor for many renowned multinational companies. Take the world's largest IT service provider IBM as an example. The company made the transition from a manufacturer into a service provider in the mid-1990s. In 2001, revenue from services reached USD 34.9 billion, accounting for 42% of the total revenue; for the first time, services replaced hardware sales to become the top revenue source for IBM. In 2005, the share of services further climbed to over 50% of the company revenue.

The traditional boundary between manufacturing and service industries has blurred. Leading manufacturing enterprises today are becoming more service-oriented. Manufacturing enterprises are paying greater attention to market research, product development, sales and marketing, and so on. On the other hand, many manufacturing enterprises opt for outsourcing to professional services providers in order to focus on core competences and lower costs. For instance, the Nike Company itself focuses almost exclusively on design, marketing, and advertising and outsources most of its production to third-party manufacturers globally. The outsourcing trend fosters the developments in the producer services industry such as management consulting, financial support, and logistics services.

All the trends have important implications for global supply chains. Indeed, in recent years, service-oriented supply chain operations have been thriving globally. An increasing number of enterprises in China have recognized the importance of servitization to stay competitive. Developments in producer services and service supply chains are drawing attention; however, systematic research into the service supply chains in academic circles in China remains lacking. Very few researches touch on topics such as the features of service supply chains, the supply chain topology, the interactions between service providers and users, the configuration of service supply chains, the critical factors behind service outsourcing, and the implementation of service supply chain strategy. Further, current research studies into producer services in China have not taken into account the knowledge- and information-based feature of modern supply chains, and have failed to emphasize the important integration of upstream and downstream players. The main theme of this book is modern service supply chains. This book has incorporated the major findings of "Research on Stakeholder-oriented Logistics Enterprises Performance Evaluation" (70772088) supported by the National Natural Science Foundation of China and the ongoing study "Research on the Production Services Strategy of Enterprises in China" (11XNI002) by the Renmin University of China. We believe a comprehensive investigation into modern service supply chain management is crucial for driving the development of capital- and knowledge-intensive service supply chain in China.

It is noteworthy that the "servitization of industries" and the rise of service supply chains by no means imply that the primary and secondary industries and their importance are to be replaced. In fact, the rise of producer service industry is the very result of more refined growth strategies adopted by different players in the primary and secondary industries; these industries support each other's growth. The service industry in China is less developed as compared to that in the advanced economies. To boost the developments in producer services industry and service supply chain operations, it is important to promote service outsourcing—outsourcing the non-core operations to professional service providers and accelerating the information technology (IT) services to facilitate unimpeded information flow.

In this book, we will study the importance of service-oriented supply chains for businesses today. We illustrate how integrated service providers create value for their customers. Also provided are case studies, including the experiences of Li & Fung and some leading integrated service providers in China.

Let me take this opportunity to thank Feng Zhiyan of the National Natural Science Foundation of China, and also Chang KaMun, Gordon Lam, and Natalie Leung of the Li & Fung Research Centre for their invaluable insights. I would also like to offer my sincere thanks to my teacher Professor Peng Xinlv for his great support; and my PhD student Liu Linyang, Doctor Wang Nan from the Beijing Language and Culture University, Doctor Chen Jinliang from the Central University of Finance and Economics, and Cao Qinyng of the Chinese Renmin University Press for their extensive support to this book.

Chapter 1

From Goods-Oriented Supply Chains to Service-Oriented Supply Chains

The role of the service industry has become increasingly important in the global economy. In recent years, service activities have been accounting for over 60% of the gross domestic product (GDP) on a global average; in high-income countries, the average share of services in GDP exceeds 70%. The service industry has become the major pillar of wealth creation for many economies. In 2000, the share of services in GDP was 67.1%, of which, the share of services in GDP for high-, middle-, and low-income countries was 72.4%, 55.3%, and 51.1%, respectively. In 2004, the share of services in GDP rose to 69%.

Let us first begin by describing what comprises services. There are two types of services; namely, consumer services and producer services. Consumer services are offered by providers directly to consumers, while producer services are offered to producers or other service intermediaries. Both consumer and producer services industries have grown over the years along with economic growth. The service industry has also been constantly evolving, from being labor-intensive to becoming increasingly knowledge- and human capital-intensive. We have also seen the emergence of new service sectors that cater to new demands, which has been driving the growth in the share of services in GDP.

The shift from being a manufacturing economy to a service economy has brought about sweeping changes in many companies across the globe. In recent years, many leading companies have been paying increasing attention to services, hoping to leverage on services to sustain their competitive edge. More and more companies are shifting from selling products to selling integrated products and services that deliver value. Companies with better service capabilities are generally more competitive. In fact, over the past decades, many business experts have pointed out that going forward, enterprises should adopt a service-oriented business model instead of a product-oriented one. This service-driven transformation is not only widely observed in business-to-consumer (B2C) companies such as Kodak and Apple, but can also be commonly seen in business-to-business (B2B) companies such as IBM and General Electric. Businesses are now paying increasing attention to service supply chain strategies.

Despite rising recognition of the importance of services, from both academic and practical standpoints, the focus on purchasing and supply, as well as supply chain and operations management remains largely skewed toward the manufacturing sector. This point has been highlighted in *Understanding and Managing the Services Supply Chain* (Ellram, Tate, and Billington 2004). For a long time, people have focused on supply chains for manufactured goods. Manufacturing of goods was viewed as the core activity of most companies and economies. The reasons behind the lack of attention are two-fold. First, the global economy was built on the manufacturing and farming sectors, whereas the service sector has only emerged over recent decades. Besides, the nature of services and their distinct characteristics of intangibility, simultaneity, heterogeneity, and perishability also make services difficult for people to visualize and measure. The fact that services are often not procured and managed centrally within an organization also added to the difficulty of formalizing research on service supply chain management.

The Goods-Oriented Supply Chain and Its Limitations

References to supply chain management can be traced back to literature from the 1980s. Back then, the core focus of supply chain management was on improving physical distribution, as well as striking a balance between supply and demand in order to reduce inventories. Many people viewed the concept of supply chain management to be the same as that of logistics, or at best, an extension of logistics. The early supply chain management idea was primarily concerned with the retail and grocery industry, as this industry often bears a higher level of inventories.

Today, however, there is general consensus that supply chain management encompasses a broader concept as compared to logistics management. As reflected upon by Cooper, Lambert, and Pagh in *Supply Chain*

Management: More Than a New Name for Logistics (1997, 1–14), there is a need for some level of coordination of activities and processes within and between organizations in the supply chain that extends beyond logistics. For instance, when developing new products, companies need to coordinate activities such as research and development, sales and marketing, manufacturing, financing, and so on. Handfield and Nichols (1999) shared a similar view and defined supply chain as "encompassing all activities associated with the flow and transformation of goods from the raw material stage, to the end users, as well as the associated information flow. Material and information flow both up and down the supply chain. Supply chain management is the integration of these activities through improved supply chain relationships so as to achieve a sustainable competitive advantage."

As can be seen, the current popular notion of supply chain is goods-oriented. Goods are the primary unit of exchange, and physical movement of goods is considered the core activity of most companies. Supply chain management concerns getting the right products delivered to the right place at the right time; this involves activities such as supplier selection and logistics management. In this respect, it can be said that services such as inventory management in supply chain management are subordinate to goods flows; they can be considered as induced activities of goods-oriented supply chains, aiming to improve the efficiency and effectiveness in product distribution. Using the language in resources management theory, goods-oriented supply chains place heavy emphasis on "operand" resources—resources that must be acted upon to be beneficial and are usually finite and in tangible and static forms. On the other hand, "operant" resources that act upon other resources to create benefits such as knowledge, skills, and capabilities receive scant attention in contrast (Vargo and Lusch 2008).

Besides, a goods-oriented supply chain often implies a sequential architecture linking upstream and downstream players. A goods-oriented supply chain has traditionally been presented as a linear, sequential set of functions: product development, procurement, manufacturing, storage, distribution, and sales. Supply chain management concerns both inter- and intra-firm coordination of physical, capital, and information flows between suppliers, manufacturers, distributors, and retailers. To ensure effective integration, traditional manufacturing and other supply chain activities are often closely knitted and geographically colocated. Excessive geographical dispersion in supply chain activities is considered to bring additional production risks and operating costs.

Further, in goods-oriented supply chains, be it a pull-driven, push-driven, or push-pull kind of system, value is considered to be created by a single side—the producers. Customers, though the initiators of demand, do not play any role in supply chain activities and are solely the recipients of goods. Producers create value-in-exchange.

Although a goods-oriented approach takes on a holistic and systemic view to analyze different supply chain activities, it has several major limitations. First, a goods-oriented approach tends to see things from the standpoint of manufacturers and pays little attention to the unique value created by services. Second, although information sharing is emphasized in goods-oriented supply chains, knowledge creation and transmission via information exchange is often overlooked. Third, the traditional sequential nature of goods-oriented supply chains imposes constraints on innovations and the development potential of companies. Indeed, over the past decade, we have witnessed significant changes in supply chain configurations—a multitude of activities now often take place simultaneously in a supply chain to enhance responsiveness to the rapidly changing consumer demand. Fourth, goods-oriented supply chain strategies, which can be easily replicated, are widely known and practiced by many companies today. The marginal benefits to companies yielded by adopting goods-oriented supply chain strategies are diminishing.

Indeed, the basic supply chain processes have, in recent times, evolved from ones that are sequential and geographically concentrated to ones that are highly dynamic and more open. Remarkable advances in information technologies and global logistics have made dispersed manufacturing a reality. The assembly of the Boeing's 777 jet described in *Competing in the Flat World* (Fung, Fung, and Wind 2009) is a case in point. The Boeing's 777 jet is assembled from three million parts sourced from over 900 suppliers from 17 countries. Boeing was responsible for manufacturing mainly the wings and fuselage, as well as assembling the aircraft; and it outsourced most of the plane's components to suppliers around the world. For Boeing 787, the company also outsourced the systems for collision avoidance and landing in zero visibility to Indian engineers at HCL Technologies outside New Delhi. Dispersed manufacturing allows Boeing to find the best-in-class suppliers for each component and helps it diversify risks and make global sales.

We have witnessed a rise in global supply networks over the past few years. The traditional sequential supply chains have been fragmented into different process modules that can be dispersed across the globe. Different modules in a supply network interact dynamically, often in a non-sequential manner, with one another to realize value creation. Capability to create value through collaboration and integration in global supply network today holds the key to success. Indeed, competition today is increasingly "network against network," rather than on a "firm against firm" basis.

The modularization of supply network processes includes not only traditional activities such as raw material supply, manufacturing, wholesale and retail, and customer services, but also extends to high value-added activities critical to company competiveness such as design, technological applications, and financial services. The flow and integration of knowledge and technology play an increasingly important role in building a successful supply network. By focusing solely on the coordination of manufacturing activities, a traditional goods-oriented supply chain management approach would clearly fail to accommodate these important changes. A new approach that pays better attention to unbundling supply chains and capturing and creating value through the integration of different process modules in supply networks is needed (Exhibit 1.1).

Apart from the rise of supply networks, the breaking down of the boundaries of different industries also poses another challenge to using a goods-oriented supply chain approach in analyzing business activities. Over the past decades, we have observed the increasing number of connections and integration of different industries, such as the emergence of logistics finances, technology finances, and energy finances, which has fundamentally changed the way businesses create value. Many manufacturers have formed collaborative networks with logistics and distribution enterprises; the traditional sequential supply chain approach fails to explain and incorporate these new dynamics.

Last but not least, consumer behavior has been rapidly changing over the past decades. In the past, consumers were passive recipients of products and services; they merely bought and consumed what producers created. However, the growing trends of experiential marketing and operations suggest that consumers now play a more active role—the value of goods and services can be cocreated through the interaction of consumers and producers (Exhibit 1.2). In fact, marketing experts have pointed out that enterprises cannot deliver value independently but can only offer value propositions to consumers. Enterprises can offer their goods and services for value creation, and collaboratively create value-in-use only with the acceptance of value propositions by consumers (Grönroos 2000). This is completely different from the goods-oriented supply chain approach, which sees that value is singly created by producers, and this has far-reaching implications on supply chain configurations.

Exhibit 1.1: Changing Service Supply Chain Processes

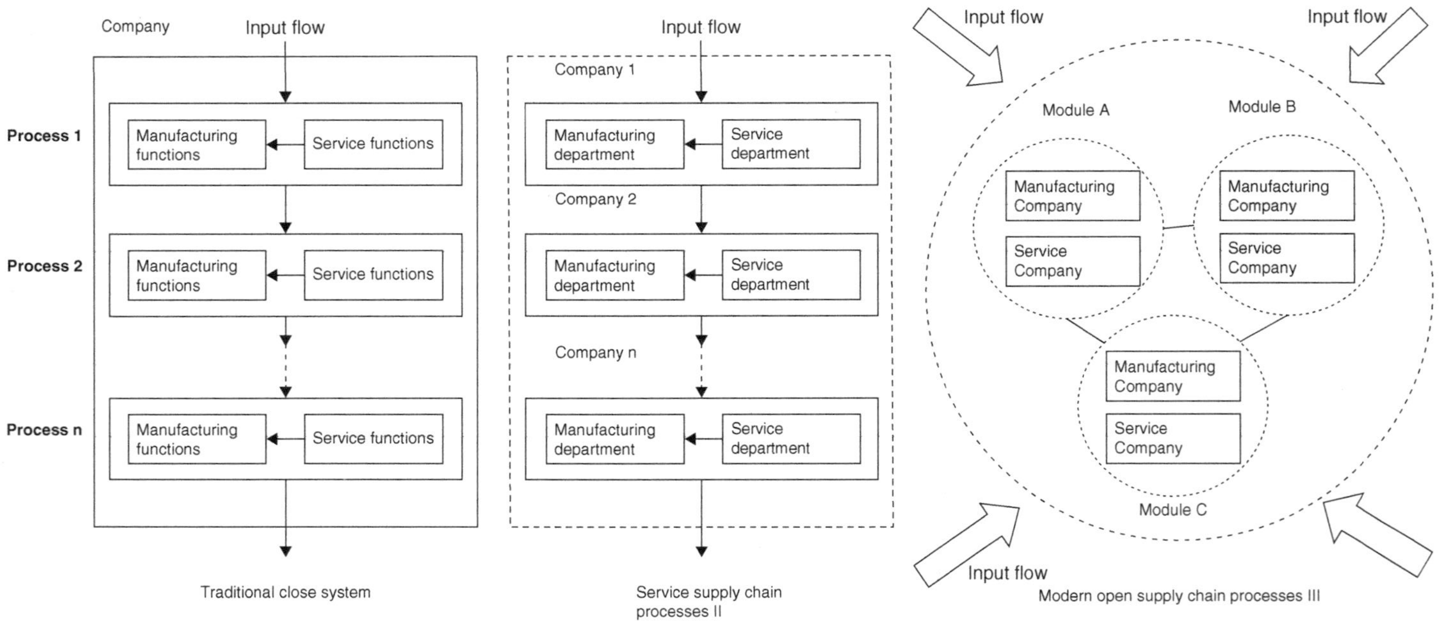

Exhibit 1.2: Cocreation of Value by Both Producers and Customers

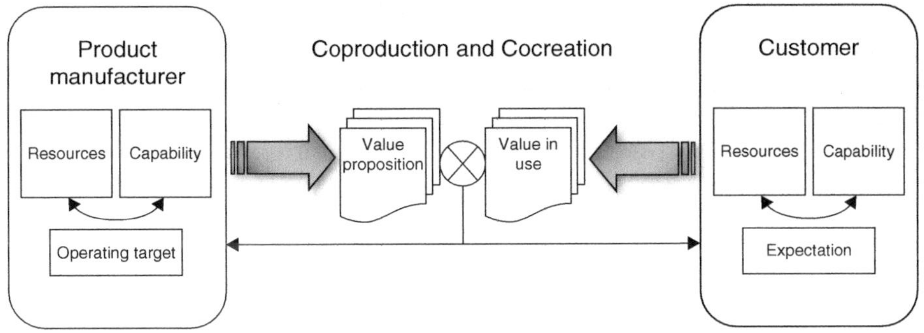

Seeing the many limitations of a goods-oriented supply chain approach, Vargo and Lusch (2008) put forward a new service-oriented approach to incorporate prominent changes such as the modularization of supply chain processes, the breaking down of boundaries of different industries, and the rise of experiential operations. The new approach has eight foundational premises: (1) the application of specialized skills and knowledge is the fundamental unit of exchange; (2) indirect exchange masks the fundamental unit of exchange; (3) goods are distribution mechanisms for service provision; (4) knowledge is the fundamental source of competitive advantage; (5) all economies are service economies; (6) the customer is always a coproducer; (7) the enterprise can only make value proposition; and (8) a service-centered view is customer-oriented and relational.

The Service-Oriented Supply Chain

More and more companies now recognize the value of services in supply chain management. Service-oriented supply chains are gaining attention. But, what exactly is a service-oriented supply chain? Although academicians have differing views about service-oriented supply chains, we can classify them into three schools of thought:

1. A service supply chain concerns only the service-related activities in a supply chain; managing these activities help companies achieve the best service at lowest costs. For instance, de Waart and Kemper (2004, 30–5) defined a service supply chain to include all processes and activities

involved in the planning, movement, and repair of materials to enable after-sales support of the company's products. On that basis, they suggested five steps to achieve service chain excellence, so that companies can achieve an optimal trade-off between cost or inventory investment and service level. Youngdahl and Loomba (2000) and Saccani, Johansson, and Perona (2007) also examined the role of service and after-sales services in global supply chain management. In China, most scholars have focused on the role of logistics in supply chains.

2. Distinguishing between services and manufacturing, the second school of thought concerns the supply chain of the service sectors, and looks at the similarities and differences of a product-based model and a service-based model so as to develop a new supply chain model specific to the service sector. In *Understanding and Managing the Services Supply Chain*, Ellram, Tate, and Billington (2004) stressed the importance of supply chain management of the service sectors. They espoused that the inherent differences in services make it necessary to have supply chain management tools specific to the service sector. Similarly, Sengupta, Heiser, and Cook (2006) conducted a comparative analysis on manufacturing and service supply chains, highlighting the differential impacts of information sharing, long-term relationship, supplier and distribution network, advanced planning systems on operational, and financial performances of companies in both the service and manufacturing sectors. They suggested that the supply chain model in the manufacturing sector cannot be directly extrapolated to service supply chains. In China, many scholars have studied the supply chains in service sectors such as aviation and tourism.

   As can be observed, the definition of services in the first school of thought is essentially the same as that of the traditional goods-oriented supply chain, that is, services are viewed as an auxiliary element in the goods manufacturing process. The second school of thought, on the other hand, goes to another extreme and excludes any elements of manufacturing activities in the service-oriented supply chains. Obviously, both schools of thoughts have their own constraints. On the one hand, the unique value created through the dynamic interactions between services and other supply chain activities are neglected. On the other hand, they fail to acknowledge the growing integration of the manufacturing and service sectors.

   Therefore, we opt for the definition of service supply chain by the third school of thought, which highlights the dynamic interactions between services and other supply chain activities.

3. Scholars of different academic backgrounds have contributed to, and enriched the understanding of service supply chains in this school.

For instance, the well-known service-dominant logic put forward by Vargo and Lusch (2008) in the field of marketing argues that service is the basis of all exchanges; in fact, service is exchanged for service. Market players, through the application of operant resources (knowledge and skills), interact with one another to provide services. Sometimes, the interactions involve physical goods and manufacturing activities, but goods should be considered the transmitters of operant resources (embedded knowledge). In the field of economics, Greenfield (1966) was the first to introduce the concept of producer services in his study of the service sector and its classifications. Later, Hansen (1994) suggested that producer services are service inputs in manufacturing or other service processes to create value and enhance operating efficiency in different stages of production, including both upstream and downstream activities. Juleff (1996) claimed that producer services are primarily dependent upon the manufacturing sector to provide a demand for their output. In operations management, the earliest usage of the terms "servitization" and "service manufacturing" come from Van der Merwe and Rada (1988). They suggested that companies can add value to their core corporate offerings through services. Modern corporations increasingly provide comprehensive market packages, which bundle customer-focused combinations of goods, services, support, self-service, and knowledge; services are playing a dominant role today.

In this book, we amalgamate the concepts of services in various fields in our understanding of service-oriented supply chains. When a customer places a service request to an integrated service provider, the latter will consolidate the operant and operand resources to provide a service solution. When needed, the integrated service provider may unbundle the customer's service request, outsource the work to other indirect service providers and manage the working relationships by itself (Exhibit 1.3). There are several key points to our understanding of service-oriented supply chains. First, instead of investigating only the service activities in goods manufacturing, or focusing on merely the service sector, the service-oriented supply chain focuses on the interaction, resource integration, and cocreation of value by different market players. Service is the key driver of management and operations of supply chains. To some extent, we can say that the service-oriented supply chain extends the customer-oriented concept in modern supply chain management, which strives to satisfy the diverse demands of customers through services. Second, the integrated service provider plays a crucial role in constructing and managing the entire service supply chain; through demand forecasting and customer relationship

Exhibit 1.3: A Service-Oriented Supply Chain

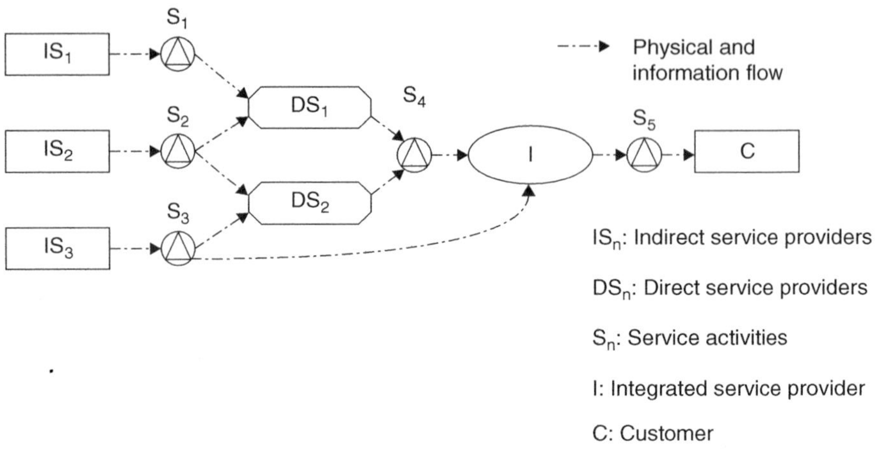

management, the integrated service provider gauges and grasps the changes in demand, and continuously seeks new growth points in value creations. Third, through performance evaluations and supplier management, the integrated service provider consolidates the resources of both the direct and indirect service providers, and offers value-added services to its customers. The integrated service providers construct a network with service activities that are the "nodes" for physical and information flows.

Case Study: Flextronics: Designing a Service Supply Chain for a Renowned Mobile Phone Company in China

Headquartered in Singapore, Flextronics is a leading electronics manufacturing service (EMS) provider that offers end-to-end creative design, manufacturing, and logistics services to automobiles, industrial manufacturing, and medical and technology companies. Flextronics manufactures a wide range of hi-tech products such as mobile phones, computers, and routers, to many Fortune 500 companies including Hewlett-Packard, Sony Ericsson, and Nokia. The company designs, manufactures, transports, and offers after-sales services to its customers with its global network of factory facilities in more than 30 countries. Through its vertically integrated electronics manufacturing services, Flextronics helps its customers lower costs and reduce lead time. In 2010, the company revenue reached USD 24,110.7 million.

China is the world's largest mobile telecommunications market. With rapid advancement in wireless technology and consistent growth in the number of mobile phone users, China's mobile phone industry has been growing at a stunning rate. Today, the Asian markets account for 46% of the revenue of Flextronics, and China contributes to half of the share. By industry, mobile phone manufacturing accounts for 31% of the revenue of Flextronics. On account of winning huge number of outsourced manufacturing orders from Ericsson, Alcatel, Nokia, and Motorola, Flextronics is regarded as the world factory for mobile phones. Company N, a renowned international mobile phone manufacturer, is one of the most important customers of Flextronics. Company N is influential in the research and development of wireless technology applications. Flextronics is the original design manufacturer (ODM) partner of Company N; it offered electronics manufacturing services to Company N for the China market. In other words, Company N outsourced its entire supply chain from product development to retail distribution to Flextronics.

Before outsourcing to Flextronics, the mobile phone supply chain of Company N in China involved three major stages: product development, manufacturing, and distribution (Exhibit 1.4).

Exhibit 1.4: The Previous Supply Chain of Company N

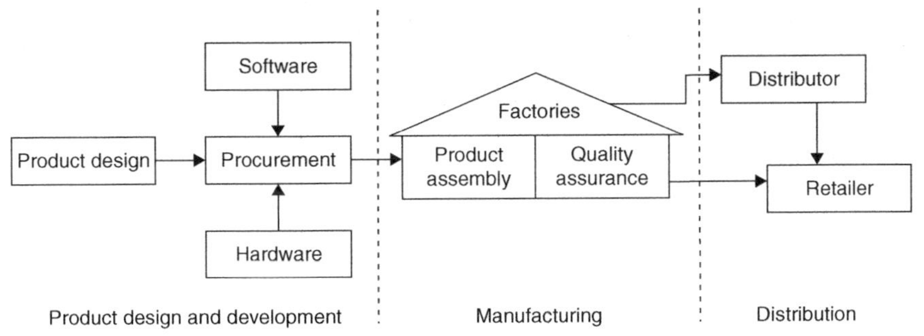

Product design and parts procurement are the two important activities in product development. Company N encountered several country-specific challenges during this stage in China. On the one hand, product life cycle in China's mobile phone market is very short. In order to respond to the rapidly changing market demand, Company N needed to frequently launch new phone models to maintain its leadership position. Based on the statistics collected by Flextronics, Company N introduced new phone models every quarter. On the other hand, China's mobile phone parts suppliers are mostly small in size and geographically scattered; this poses difficulty for Company N to consolidate its supplier base to enhance efficiency and build long-term partnerships. Product assembly and quality assurance are two important stages in product manufacturing. The state-of-the-art assembly line of Company N is highly efficient. That said, no company can win in China by relying solely on advanced technology. Company N faced a challenge in making good use of the abundant resources and localizing its operations in China. Last but not least, Company N also needed to strike a balance between efficiency and operating costs in retail distribution in China.

Taking into account the features of the mobile phone supply chain as well as the bottlenecks faced by Company N in China, Flextronics designed the service supply chain for Company N (Exhibit 1.5).

In the newly designed service supply chain for Company N, Flextronics offers end-to-end solutions to integrate upstream and downstream resources and capabilities. As an integrated service provider, Flextronics unbundles the customer request and might outsource the service activities to third-party service providers. Flextronics takes the lead in integrating the upstream and downstream resources and manages the core supply chain activities.

With over 6,000 product design engineers, Flextronics has leading design capability and offers a wide range of global product design solutions to cater to diverse consumer demands, with services including integrated circuit design, accessories and software design, testing, and so on. Designers in Flextronics are responsible for designing phone models, and the company evaluates the design concepts based on functionalities, consistency, aesthetics, and so on to assess if further improvements are needed. Once the designs are approved, Flextronics acquires the necessary software and parts.

Mobile phone software plays a key role in consumer experience. For this part, Flextronics has two options: develop its own software or outsource software development to third-party software providers. Flextronics and Company N opt for codeveloping the core software, and outsourcing the less important ones. As finding the right software providers is often difficult, Flextronics spends a huge amount of time and effort in software procurement, and strives to develop close and long-term partnerships with the right software providers. As for hardware procurement, Flextronics fully utilizes the potential of the abundant number of suppliers in China and has built two industrial parks in China. By having suppliers colocate their industrial parks, Flextronics achieves zero inventories and enhances product quality due to better communications with suppliers. Time-to-market is shortened

Exhibit 1.5: The Service Supply Chain for Company N

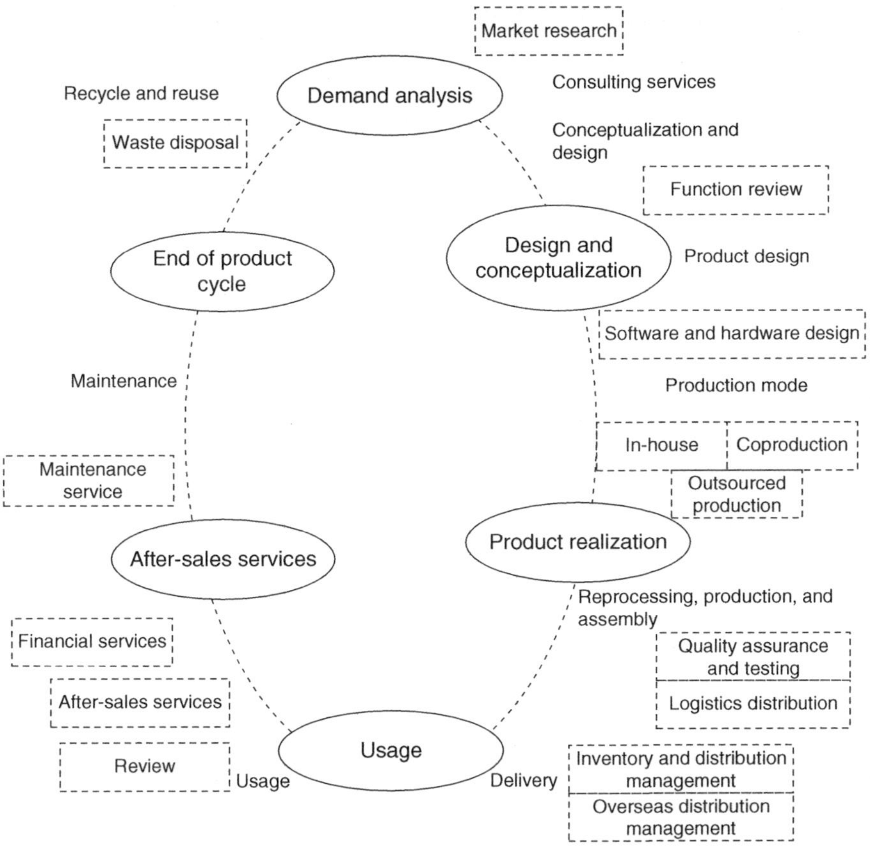

with reductions in logistics costs. For instance, the Zhuhai Industrial Park houses suppliers of mobile phone accessories such as cases, printed circuit boards (PCBs), cameras, keyboards, and liquid crystal displays (LCDs).

The next process is product assembly. Local manufacturers in Shenzhen are responsible for most of this process. After assembly, the mobile phones are fully tested and examined with a series of quality assurance procedures before being sold in the market. Depending on the size of orders and geographical locations, the products are transported either by road or air. Most often, the products are distributed to the regional distribution centers of retailers, before being sent to sub-distributors. On the other hand, some products may be distributed through direct-to-retail arrangements.

The competitiveness of Flextronics lies in its ability to efficiently collect and analyze the information of the entire service supply chain, and through which the company can achieve effective demand management, relationship management, and service management. By establishing close relationships with Company N and its suppliers, Flextronics designs and manages the service supply chain for Company N, and can deliver the products without the participation of any third parties. Upon receiving the demand forecasts from Company N through the BizTalk Server, Flextronics works with Company N, its production team, and suppliers to develop the manufacturing plan, and all data will be imported into the enterprise resource planning (ERP) system and stored in a central database.

Flextronics offers total services solutions for Company N from product design, batch production, quality assurance, distribution to after-sales services.

Features of Service-Oriented Supply Chains

There are key differences between service-oriented and goods-oriented supply chains, as illustrated in Exhibit 1.6.

Exhibit 1.6: Goods-Oriented vs. Service-Oriented Supply Chains

	Goods-oriented supply chain	Service-oriented supply chain
Primary unit of exchange	Materials and goods	Services
Determination of value	Determined singly by producers	Determined by both sides
Role of customers	Passive recipients of goods	Coproducers of services
Goal of supply chain operations	Customer satisfaction	Customer success
Supply chain configuration	Sequential and linear	Chain-, radiation-, or star-shaped network
Focus on resource consolidation	Operand resources	Operant resources

First, service is the primary unit of exchange in service-oriented supply chains. As in the case of Flextronics, the company not only engages in original equipment manufacturing (OEM), but also plays a key role in developing the original design manufacturing (ODM) and the supplier system. Although several physical and manufacturing activities are involved, services and the differentiated service system is the fundamental source of value creation.

Second, in service-oriented supply chains, the service providers work together with their customers to create value. In the example of Flextronics, the company collaborates, communicates, and works together with its customers throughout the entire supply chain process, including concept formulations, design, production, distribution, and after-sales activities. Close interactions with the customers allow service providers to cater to the unique and ever-changing customer demand.

Third, the goal of service-oriented supply chain operations is customer success, instead of customer satisfaction as in the case of goods-oriented supply chain operations. The latter implies that the levels of customer expectations can be pre-specified, and service providers have to meet or exceed the targets with various management methods. However, achieving customer success needs a different approach. Service providers strive to develop long-term strategic partnership with their customers to gain a deep understanding of the operations, and constantly explore new operating models for their customers to bring future success.

Fourth, service-oriented supply chains are open, dynamic, and adaptive, rather than sequential and static. The service-oriented supply chains have configurations that foster learning and exchanges. Service-oriented supply chains emphasize interactions with external parties, and players constantly explore and acquire new capabilities and knowledge to seek new opportunities and system-wide improvements.

Fifth, unlike goods-oriented supply chains, service-oriented supply chains target integration of intangible operant resources (knowledge, skills, and capabilities) and view them as a major source for value creation. Goods, on the other hand, are operand resources. They are viewed as transmitters of operant resources (embedded knowledge), which plays a much less important role in value creation.

Chapter 2
The Topological Structures of Service Supply Chains

As discussed in Chapter 1, there are many key differences between service-oriented and goods-oriented supply chains. These differences undoubtedly have important implications on service supply chain topologies,[1] that is, the patterns of interconnections between different elements such as links and nodes in service networks. Despite the growing importance of service supply chains to company competiveness, academic investigation into service supply chains remains largely unexplored, with most studies focused on conceptualizing the idea of service supply chains. There are very few studies on the topologies of service supply chains. In this chapter, we will investigate the different topologies of service-oriented supply chains.

The Evolution of Service-Oriented Supply Chain Management Models

The concept of service supply chains is relatively new, complex, and evolving. For a long time, goods-oriented supply chains have grabbed major attention in academic circles. This explains the strong influence of goods-oriented supply chain frameworks observed in studies on service supply chains. To begin with, let us briefly study the evolution of different supply chain models.

[1] Topology has its roots in computer network studies. It refers to the layout pattern of interconnections of different elements (links, nodes, and so on) in a network. Topology can be understood as the shape or structure of a network, and it is not concerned with the actual physical design of the elements in the network. Any particular network topology is determined only by the graphical mapping of the configuration of physical and/or logical connections between nodes. Distances between nodes, physical interconnections, and so on, may differ in two networks and yet have identical topologies.

Hewlett-Packard (HP) Supply Chain Management Model

The HP supply chain management model, one of the earliest models, is based on the supply chain operations initiatives of HP in the late 1980s (Lee and Billington 1995). During that period, HP faced the double challenge of climbing inventory costs and alarming customer dissatisfaction with its order fulfilment. The production bases and research and development (R&D) centers of HP were spread across 16 countries; its sales and service centers, across 110 countries. Offering over 22,000 types of products, the complicated operation processes of R&D, production, and sales centers resulted in bottlenecks in its product supply chains, thereby adversely affecting customer satisfaction. Although HP had tried to increase its inventory levels to meet customer demand, the efforts proved futile with the ever-expanding and increasingly diverse customer needs. To resolve these problems, the company management remodeled its supply chains and built new warehouses for inventory stockpiles at different strategic stages of the supply chains (Exhibit 2.1). The remodeling efforts greatly enhanced customer satisfaction and helped HP lower its inventory costs. As a result, HP enjoyed impressive improvements in its profit margins.

The HP supply chain management model treats the supply chain as a production and distribution network, which mainly involves transforming the raw materials into semi-finished products and then final products, and distributing the final products to customers. Core supply chain activities include procurement, manufacturing, distribution, and so on.

Exhibit 2.1: The Remodeled HP Supply Chain in the 1980s

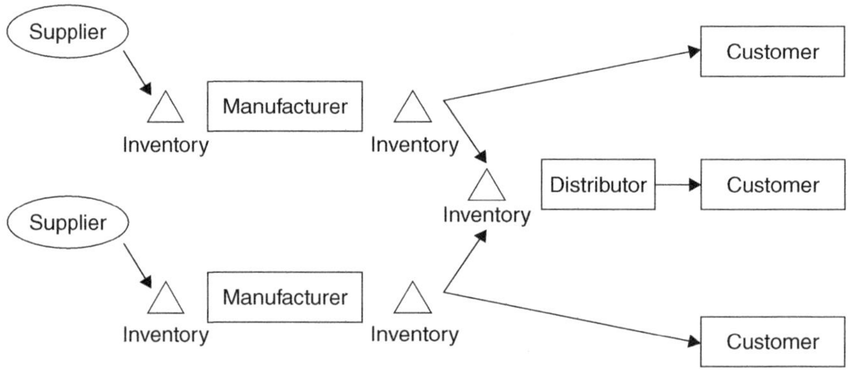

Source: Lee and Billington (1995).

Supply Chain Operations Reference (SCOR) Supply Chain Management Model

The SCOR model is a process reference model developed in 1996 by two management consulting firms in Boston—Pittiglio Rabin Todd and McGrath (PRTM) and AMR Research. The SCOR model was endorsed by the Supply Chain Council (SCC) as the cross-industry de-facto standard diagnostic tool for supply chain management. It is the first standard supply chain reference framework that links business processes, metrics, best practices, and technology features into a unified structure to support communication among supply chain partners so that users can objectively address and improve the effectiveness of supply chain management and related supply chain improvement activities.

The SCOR model provides three levels of process details. They assist companies in defining: scope (Level 1), configuration or type of supply chain (Level 2), and process element details, including performance attributes (Level 3). There can be other levels below level 3, in which companies further fragment process elements specific to their own needs; however, these process details are not included in the framework of the SCOR model.

SCOR Level 1

Level 1 is the highest level of the SCOR model. It defines the scope and content of the supply chains based on the strategic objectives of companies, and provides a basis for setting the competition performance targets. SCOR Level 1 has five basic management processes: plan, source, make, deliver, and return.

SCOR Level 2

Level 2 is made up of different process categories that determine the configuration of a supply chain. Companies implement their operations strategies through different planning, source, make, deliver, and return processes. These selections will have an impact on SCOR Level 3 processes, which are the business activities within a configuration.

For instance, a manufacturing company can have many different production approaches: make-to-stock, make-to-order, make-to-assemble, or customized production. Once the process categories are confirmed, companies can determine the configurations of their supply chains, such as the physical layouts of the supply chain partners (e.g., customers, suppliers, warehouses, factories, and order centers) and the directions of information and physical flows.

SCOR Level 3

Level 3 presents detailed process elements information for each Level 2 process category and completes the SCOR framework. Level 3 also identifies the best practices (if applicable), process performance metrics, and the system capabilities required to support the best practices. Therefore, Level 3 defines a company's ability to compete successfully in specific markets.

The SCOR model allows businesses to describe their process architecture in a way that is commonly understood. In contrast to the HP model, the SCOR model presents a more detailed illustration of different activities in business processes, and the relationship between upstream and downstream players in a supply chain.

Global Supply Chain Forum (GSCF) Supply Chain Management Model

The GSCF introduced another supply chain framework, the GSCF supply chain model. The GSCF viewed supply chain management as the integration of key business processes from end user to suppliers providing products, services, and information that add value for customers and other stakeholders.

The GSCF supply chain management model is built on eight key business processes: customer relationship management, customer service management, demand management, order fulfilment, manufacturing flow management, product development, commercialization, and return (Exhibit 2.2).

Customer relationship management

The customer relationship management process provides a basic framework on how to develop and maintain relationships with customers. After identifying the core customer segments, the goal is to increase customer loyalty by offering customized products and services. Detailed information of relevant strategic and operational sub-processes will also be described.

Customer service management

Customer service management represents a company's window to customers. It concerns administering product and service agreements (PSAs) developed by customer teams as part of the customer relationship management process. Customer service management requires a real-time system to respond quickly to customers' requests and demands.

Demand management

Demand management seeks to balance the customers' requirements with the capabilities of the supply chain. With the right demand management process in place, company management can proactively match supply with demand and avoid any disruptions during executions.

Exhibit 2.2: The GSCF Supply Chain Management Model

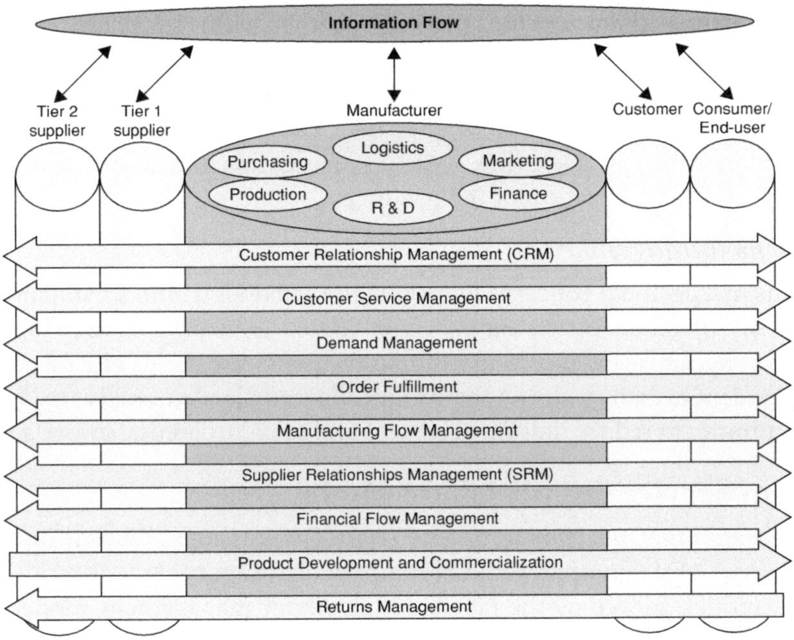

Source: Lambert, Cooper, and Pagh (1998).

Order fulfillment

Order fulfillment concerns designing a network and a process so that customers' orders can be filed efficiently and effectively, and at the same time, the total delivery costs can be minimized.

Manufacturing flow management

Manufacturing flow management is the supply chain management process that includes all activities necessary to obtain, implement, and manage manufacturing flexibility, and to move products through the manufacturing plants. Manufacturing flexibility is reflected in the ability of a company to manufacture a variety of products in a timely manner at the lowest possible cost.

Supplier relationship management

The supplier relationship management process provides an operational framework for developing and maintaining relationships with suppliers. Companies develop close rapports with a small set of key suppliers based on the value that the suppliers create over time and maintain more traditional relationships with the others.

Product development and commercialization

Product development and commercialization is the supply chain management process that offers an operational framework for developing new products and launching them in the market together with suppliers. Effective implementation of the process does not only enable company management to coordinate the flow of new products efficiently across the supply chain but also draws together other supply chain members to improve operating performance in manufacturing, logistics, marketing, and so on, in order to support commercialization of the products.

Returns management

Returns management concerns managing the activities within a company and across key members of the supply chain related to returns, reverse logistics, gate keeping, and avoidance. Successful implementation of this process enables management to manage the reverse product flow efficiently, as well as to identify opportunities to reduce unwanted returns and to control reusable assets.

Ellram Service Supply Chain Model

In *Understanding and Managing the Service Supply Chain*, Ellram, Tate, and Billington (2004) compared the HP supply chain management model, the SCOR model, as well as the GSCF supply chain management model, and analyzed the pros and cons of applying these directly to the service supply chains (Exhibit 2.3).

They pointed out that all three supply chain models are goods-oriented—they are focused on depicting the physical flow of goods along a supply chain. In essence, the three models define supply chain management as the management of information, processes, goods, and funds from the earliest supplier to the ultimate customer. However, this goods-oriented notion must be modified if the models are used to depict service supply chain. Indeed, there are some fundamental differences between goods and services that render the models unfit for describing service supply chains. For instance, services cannot be inventoried (HP model) and there is no return cycle in service provision (the SCOR model and the GSCF supply chain management model). Therefore, Ellram, Tate, and Billington extended the supply chain management concept and defined it as the management of information, processes, capacity, service performance, and funds from the earliest supplier to the ultimate customer. The service supply chain management model put forward by these authors encompasses information flow management, capacity and skills management, demand management, customer relationship management, supplier relationship management, service delivery management, and cash flow management (Exhibit 2.4).

It is noteworthy that in the service supply chain management model put forward by Ellram, Tate, and Billington (2004), capacity, which is defined as

Exhibit 2.3: Comparison of the HP Supply Chain Model, the SCOR Model, and the GSCF Model

	Concept	Areas of Focus	Pros	Cons
The HP supply chain management model	1. Suppliers, manufacturing plants, and customers are all linked in the flow of goods in an uncertain environment 2. Multiple warehouses for inventory stockpile to provide the buffer against uncertainties	1. Depicts the physical flow of goods among supply chain members 2. Focuses on recognizing and managing uncertainty 3. Uncertainty is represented by statistical variances	1. Considers buffers against uncertainty 2. Enhances capacity levels and flexibility through inventory 3. Takes into consideration the trade-off in lost sales and inventory cost	1. Services cannot be inventoried 2. Cannot address the differences in the quality of services
The SCOR model	1. Utilizes business processes and their linkages with one another to describe a supply chain 2. Organized around five primary management processes of plan, source, make, deliver, and return	1. Focuses on processes that link the supply chain 2. Describes the physical flow of goods among supply chain members	1. Services are process driven	1. The separate processes of make, deliver, and return do not apply to services 2. Services do not have a return cycle

(Continued)

Exhibit 2.3: Comparison of the HP Supply Chain Model, the SCOR Model, and the GSCF Model (*Continued*)

	Concept	Areas of Focus	Pros	Cons
The GSCF supply chain management model	1. Conceptualizes a supply chain that includes three elements: the business processes, the management components, and the structure of the chain 2. Product and processes flow in both directions through the chain, taking into account the return process flow	1. Focuses on processes that link the supply chain 2. Describes the physical flow of goods among supply chain members from supplier's supplier to end consumers	1. Participants in the entire supply chain including suppliers as well as customers 2. Coordination of information and integration to improve the overall flow of the chain 3. Utilizes a process view to meet uncertain demands	1. Services do not have a return cycle 2. Fits only the product and component flow of goods

Source: Ellram and Billington (2004).

Exhibit 2.4: Ellram Service Supply Chain Model

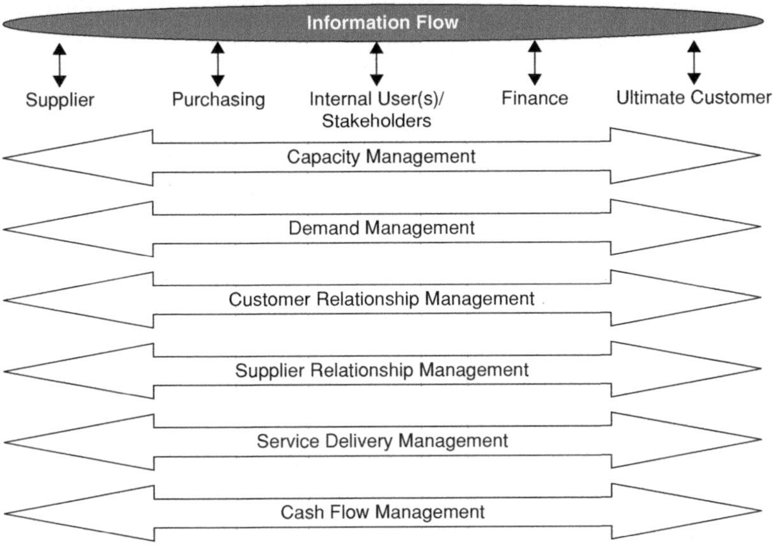

the supplier's ability to produce in order to meet the customer's needs, has an equivalent position as inventory in goods-oriented supply chains—capacity and inventory can both serve as buffer, which allows supply chains to respond to changing customer demand more quickly and with a greater level of flexibility.

Baltacioglu Service Supply Chain Model

Baltacioglu et al. (2007) studied healthcare services and developed a new model for service supply chains. The service supply chain is defined as a network of suppliers, service providers, customers, and other supporting units that perform the function of transaction of resources required to produce services followed by the transformation of these resources into supporting and core services and finally, the delivery of these services to customers. Service supply chain management are initiatives to manage the information, resources, processes, service performance, and so on, from the earliest supplier to the ultimate customer; it involves several activities, which are demand management, capacity and resources management, supplier relationship management, service performance management, order process management, customer relationship management, and information and technology management.

Demand management chiefly concerns estimating and managing customer demand to make operational decisions based on supply chain information. Capacity and resource management aims to balance customers' need and company's capacity to provide resources in order to satisfy customers' demand. Supplier relationship management's basic goal is to arrange and manage various supply sources for different goods and services, which involves supplier evaluation, negotiation with suppliers, and building supplier relationships. Service performance management, on the other hand, is the core function in the service supply chain. Because of the very nature of service businesses, the service production process requires the presence of both customers and service providers. Service performance management aims to improve the performance of service providers. Order process management involves getting orders from customers, checking the order status, communicating with customers about them, and actually fulfilling the orders. Customer relationship management focuses on the interface between the company and its customers, and involves identifying customers and their needs, and creating new customer demand. Finally, the management of information flow plays a key role in supply chain management; effective information and technology management can improve customer satisfaction through product availability, delivery accuracy, responsiveness and flexibility, improvement through feedback, and increase sales revenue and improve operational efficiency (Exhibit 2.5).

Exhibit 2.5: Baltacioglu Service Supply Chain Model

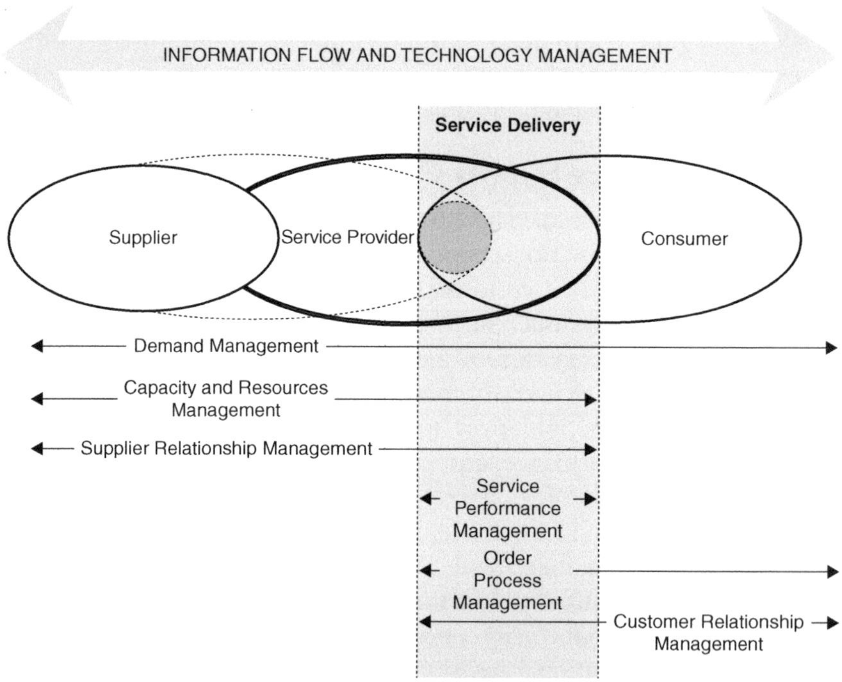

The Topological Structures, Management Processes, and Management Components of Service Supply Chains

All the five supply chain models we just discussed have taken a holistic approach in understanding supply chains. The HP supply chain management model, the SCOR model, and the GSCF supply chain management model are goods-oriented; services play only an auxiliary role to support manufacturing activities in the three models. The Ellram service supply chain model and Baltacioglu service supply chain model, in contrast, view service process as the core activity in service supply chains; however, the topological structures of service supply chains are not discussed.

For a long time, many companies viewed excellent customer services and best-in-class operation costs as two competing forces; it was assumed that companies simply cannot have the best of both worlds. However, this prevailing view has changed as an increasing number of companies have realized that they can actually profit from services (de Waart and Steve 2004). To win customers in the increasingly competitive market, many companies have made great efforts and allocated capital for their service supply chains, hoping to run their service businesses as profit centers. However, without sound knowledge of the core processes in service supply chain and their impact on service performance, many only find disproportional rewards. On this basis, a holistic and systematic approach to understanding the structure of service supply chain, the processes, and strategic components is imperative.

In this book, we share the same view as Lambert and Cooper (2000) that the formulation of a specific supply chain is determined by supply chain network structure, supply chain business process, and supply chain management component (Exhibit 2.6). The three elements are the building blocks of a theoretical framework for supply chain analysis. Supply chain network structure concerns "who the key supply chain members are and with whom to link processes"; supply chain business process concerns "what processes should be linked with each of the key supply chain members," and supply chain management components concern the "level of integration and management that should be applied for each process link."

The Topological Network Structures of Service Supply Chains

Members of a service supply chain include indirect and direct service suppliers, integrated service provider, and direct and indirect customers.

Exhibit 2.6: Elements of Supply Chain Management

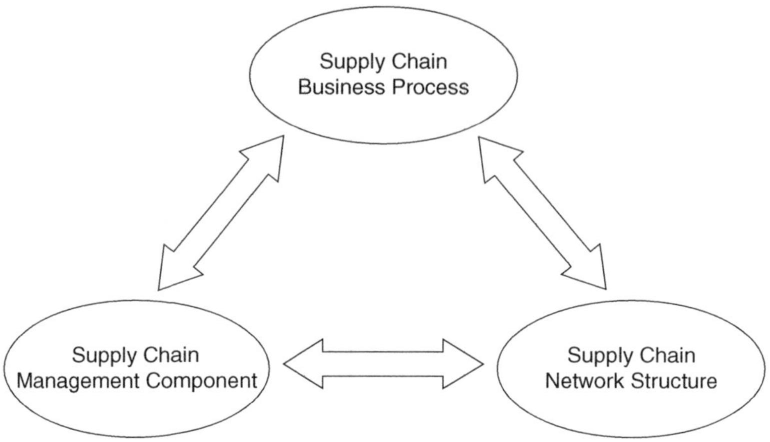

The service supply chain members are connected with one another to form a complex network through four kinds of links: managed process links, monitor process links, non-managed process links, and non-member process links (Exhibit 2.7).

Similar to product-based supply chains, service supply chains have three structural dimensions: the horizontal structure (the number of tiers across the supply chain), the vertical structure (the number of suppliers or customers represented within each tier), and the horizontal position of the integrated service provider within the end points of the supply chain. The position of the integrated service provider can be near the initial source of supply or near the end customer, or somewhere in between. While manufacturing activities and inventory serve as nodes and buffer in products-based supply chains, services and capacity serve as nodes and buffer in service supply chains.

Specifically, the topological network of a service supply chain has four characteristics. First, the topological network of a service supply chain is highly complex and may comprise product manufacturing network, logistics service network, technology service network, information network, and knowledge network. These networks interconnect with one another dynamically, and create great value for the service supply chain through interactions with customers. Second, the service supply chain members are highly diverse. They include members in traditional goods-oriented supply chain such as manufacturers, logistics companies, and customers, and also

Exhibit 2.7: Network Structure of a Service Supply Chain

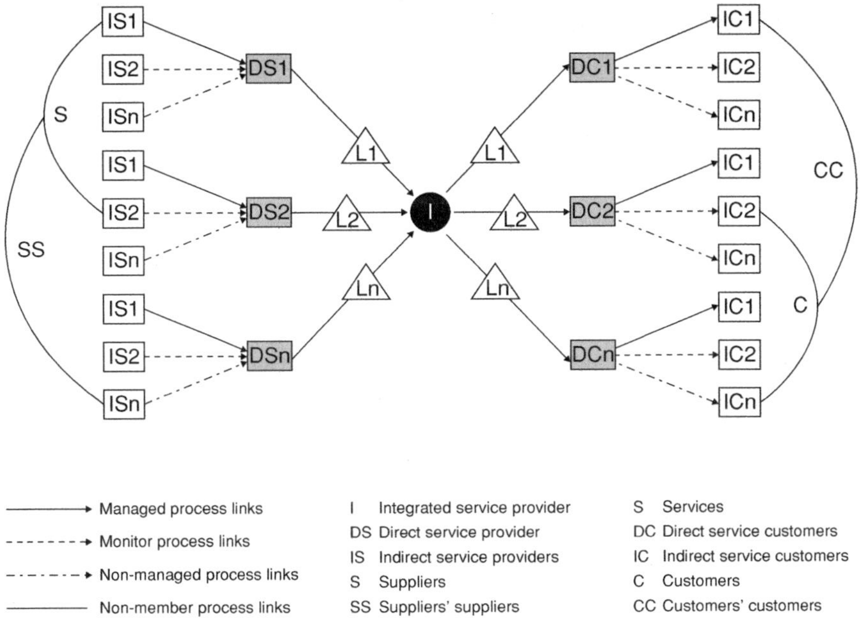

more importantly, professional service companies that do not participate in goods manufacturing and distribution, such as financial service companies, design companies, and integrated service companies. Third, the service supply chain members usually do not hold stakes in one another; they form and maintain relatively loose contractual relationships, and collaborate with one another on the basis of mutual benefits and mutual trusts. Fourth, the integrated service provider plays a leading role in construction and management of the service supply chain. It grasps changes in demand through customer demand forecasting and customer relationship management and integrates the resources and capacity of direct and indirect service providers through supplier evaluation and supplier relationship management to fulfil customers' demand. Service supply chain members connect with one another by managed process links, monitor process links, non-managed process links, and non-member process links. Through these links, the network of service supply chains can be easily extended. Effective service provision relies upon unimpeded information flow and sharing among members; it is noteworthy that some types of services must be provided alongside the physical flow of goods.

Service Supply Chain Business Process

Service supply chain management places heavy emphasis on information sharing. Apart from the support of information system and network platform, effective service supply chain management relies upon the integration and coordination of different business processes, including integrated demand management, customer relationship management, supplier relationship management, service delivery management, capacity management, fund and financing management. Some of the service supply chain processes are similar to those in goods supply chains; on the other hand, some of them are very unique.

Integrated demand management

It is the process of balancing customer demand with the supply chain capacity. Part of this process includes but goes beyond demand forecasting. It also includes efforts to synchronize market requirements and production plans. A well-executed integrated demand management can avoid uncertainty and prevent disruptions in supply chain operations.

Customer relationship management

It concerns identifying key customers and customer groups as service targets, and nurtures customer loyalty through customized products and services. In customer relationship management of service supply chains, service providers often work together with their customers to streamline business processes, eliminate low-value-added activities, formulate new process standards, and so on.

Supplier relationship management

It places emphasis on interactions with suppliers. There are three important points to note in the supplier relationship management of service supply chains. First, similar to goods supply chains, the supplier market is complex. Effective coordination of suppliers with different capabilities and resources is critical in supplier relationship management; and this requires knowledge in differentiating suppliers with different capabilities. Service providers need to consider whether to develop long-term strategic partnerships or simple transactional relationships with suppliers. Second, in service supply chain, the number of suppliers to be managed by the integrated service providers is usually bigger—the direct suppliers as well as indirect suppliers need to be monitored. Third, service providers manage not only the collaborative practices with supplier but also the collaborative relationships. Collaborative practices are a set of processes and systems that enable coordination and information sharing between the two parties which emphasize gain, often focusing on matching demand with supply. Collaborative relationships, on the other hand, place attention on long-term, mutually beneficial partnerships that focus on the needs of end customers and jointly seek to create value (Barrett and Rizza 2009).

Service delivery management

Unique to service supply chain management, service delivery management primarily concerns integrated service providers integrating and managing their back office and front office operations to deliver services effectively and efficiently in response to customer demand. Shostack (1984) suggested that service operations can be illustrated by service blueprint, which maps the sequence of events in a service and its essential functions in an objective manner. Service blueprints are often drawn to indicate which parts of the operations are visible to the customers (front office operations) and which parts of the operations are visible only to the workers (back office operations).

Capacity management

This term originated in production management, which refers to the initiatives taken by production enterprises in measuring, monitoring, and adjusting production levels, such as production planning, material demand planning, and so on, in order to manage production progress. In service supply chain management, service providers must possess adequate capacity to meet customers' demand; but at the same time, they should refrain from providing unwanted services that incur unnecessarily high costs. Adenso-Diaz (2002) pointed out that capacity management is the most difficult in the service industry. In other industries, companies can use inventories to serve as buffer; however, services can only be created and delivered simultaneously, that is, they cannot be created in advance. Besides, the intangible nature of services makes capacity management highly knowledge-intensive. It can be said that intelligence capital is at the core of capacity management in service supply chains.

Fund and financing management

It is an important management process in service supply chain management. Although integrated coordination and management of material flow, information flow, and fund flow is the key task of supply chain management, the management of fund flow is often overlooked in traditional goods supply chains. It is not uncommon to see that the reduction in costs from outsourcing to other low-cost countries is offset by increases in financing costs due to bottlenecks in fund flows. In fund and financing management, service providers strive to enhance the utilization efficiency of funds and may provide funds to companies with a shortfall of capital on the basis of effective risk management for the whole system.

Service Supply Chain Management Functions and Components

The major functions of service supply chain management are planning (value management of supply chain operations), organizing (coproduction management), coordinating (supply chain knowledge management), and control (supply chain performance and risk management).

Instead of planning for supply, production, and distribution, the focus of the planning function here refers to value management. As mentioned in Chapter 1, since companies cannot deliver value but can only offer value propositions (Vargo and Lunsh 2004), value management is an important component in service supply chain. Indeed, value is not embedded in products or services but is cocreated by service providers and customers. Scholars held different views toward value. Zeithaml (1998) viewed value as a trade-off between what is received and what is given up; Ulaga (2003) suggested that business customers value functional benefits, service benefits, and relationship benefits and would tolerate certain monetary and non-monetary sacrifices for the benefits. The changes in non-monetary sacrifices often significantly affect the strength of supply chain relationships; meanwhile, Woodruff (1997) saw value as a hierarchy of goals or desired consequences whereby supplier attributes are extremely important in facilitating goal attainments with minimal sacrifices. Value can be viewed in terms of the interactions between suppliers' products/services, customers' use situations, and customers' desired goals and end states (ibid). The above understandings of value have important implications for planning, for instance, service providers must understand desired functional, relational, and service benefits, acceptable monetary and nonmonetary sacrifices, trade-offs between benefits and sacrifices, and various use situations and conditions of the services.

Coproduction management is another component of service supply chain management. Coproduction is a complex process that creates value in use. Flint and Mentzer (2006) pointed out that customers can interact with integrated service providers to coproduce value through two primary ways, consumption and codesign. All consumers are coproducers when they interact with service providers during service provisions. Through direct feedback (e.g., customer satisfaction and direct feedback to service providers) and indirect feedback (e.g., reducing, cancelling, or increasing orders), customers influence the design and modifications of products and services. Meanwhile, the codesign of service requires customer participation in the initial design stage of service supply chains. While consumers are always coproducers of value through consumption, they are not necessarily involved in the codesign of services. Service providers must decide on the level of consumer participation in different service provisions.

Sound knowledge of global markets, different service supply chain players, and process is a prerequisite for service providers to effectively coordinate service supply chain activities. As leading players in service supply operations, integrated service providers must have a thorough understanding of customer expectations and demand levels in different countries and cultures, as well as the culture, strategies, processes, and operations of different service supply chain players. Integrated service providers must also possess strong knowledge of different processes in order to integrate across functions and companies (Flint and Mentzer 2006).

Lastly, an important component of service supply chain management is supply chain performance and risk management. Service supply chain operations integrate different types of resources and companies to form a complex network to create value for consumers. However, at the same time, these complex processes often incur risks, such as changes in supply chain structures due to changes in the operating environment and changes in value pursuits of consumers. Therefore, it is necessary to establish a sound risk management mechanism, which encompasses integrated management of service components, management of supply chain structure and relationships, as well as performance measures and management.

Chapter 3
Interactions in Service Supply Chain Operations

From our earlier discussions on different service supply chain structures, we can see that with intensifying market competition as well as increasingly diverse customer requirements, no company can accomplish all service operations without the collaborative efforts of partners, suppliers, and customers. Driven by increasing technical and logistics complexities, the rise of disperse manufacturing processes, improvements in suppliers' capability, and the considerations to lower risks and costs, an ever increasing number of companies today are opting for service outsourcing (Sturgeon and Florida 2004). Effective coordination and interactions are critical in service supply chain management (Edvardsson, Holmlund, and Strandvik 2008; Cova and Salle 2008). However, interactions in service supply chains are more complex than mere simple upstream-downstream relationships concerned only with the production and delivery of goods; as we will see later, the interdependence between different service practices and service structures forms the basis for service systems and value cocreation.

Before we study the interactions in service supply chains, let us briefly look at some generic interaction models. Hakansson (1982) proposed an interactions model (Exhibit 3.1) that identified four major elements in interactions: interaction process, interaction entities, the environment, and the atmosphere of relationship.

There are two types of interaction processes: short-term and long-term. Short-term exchanges include product-service, financial, information, and social exchanges. Over time, these exchanges may become institutionalized through contracts and adaptations to lower transaction costs and enhance efficiency. In the interactions framework, interactions between entities are affected by factors such as resources (e.g., technology and know-how),

Exhibit 3.1: The Basic Framework of Interactions Model

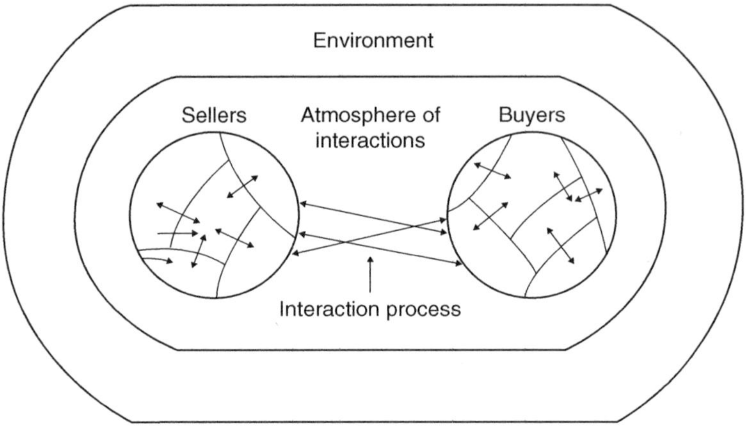

organizational characteristics (e.g., organization size and structure), and organizational experience. Besides, the interactions processes cannot be studied in isolation but must be understood in the context of the broader environment, which include several aspects: market structure (e.g., market concentration and rate of change), dynamism within relationships, internationalization, market position, and social system (e.g., language and culture). Last but not least, the atmosphere of interactions can be expressed in terms of the state of conflict or cooperation and overall closeness of the relationship. This is company-specific and is affected by the other three elements of interactions. It is very difficult to directly measure the atmosphere of interactions.

Apart from the factors mentioned by Hakansson, Hsu (2005) suggested that channel climate, environmental uncertainty, and technical dynamics would affect interactions. The level of information sharing tends to be higher in a harmonious channel climate, an uncertain environment, and in the case of greater technical dynamics. Using a managerial perspective, Ramani and Kumar (2008) suggested that factors such as reward system, dependence on patents, outsourcing experience, and institutional pressure will influence interactions. A reward system with heavier emphasis on maintaining customer relationships, lower dependence on patents, extensive outsourcing experience, and a more open institutional environment can facilitate interactions.

Interactions in Service-Oriented Supply Chains

The effectiveness of interactions has a major impact on operating performance. The previous discussions on interactions have brought to the fore different factors such as environment and atmosphere. That said, in terms of the interacting entities, there is greater focus on the interactions between suppliers and buyers, be it between companies and their suppliers, or between companies and their customers, the relationships are mostly bilateral. However, in service supply chains, integration of service elements to create value tends to involve interactions with multiple parties. Interactions in service supply chains are more complex—they go beyond interactions between upstream and downstream players.

As the operating focus shifts from product manufacturing to services in service-oriented supply chain operations, service brand is considered an important asset by many companies (Brodie, Glynn, and Little 2006). The concept of service brand was first introduced by Berry (2000), who suggested that branding is a principal success driver for service providers as it boosts customers' confidence in making invisible purchases. Bitner (1995) suggested that the process to create service brands involves three types of interactions between different entities: (1) interactions between companies and their customers, that is, making promises; (2) interactions between companies and contributors (its employees or other partners in the service network), that is, enabling and facilitating promises; and (3) interactions between contributors and the customers, that is, keeping or supporting the promise (Exhibit 3.2). On this basis, Little (2004) explored the processes of customer value creation and delivery from an organization-wide perspective. Apart from the processes of making, keeping, and enabling promises, Little added a fourth dimension, that is, realizing promise through the three aforementioned processes, which creates value for customers and financial benefits for the company. The creation of value for customers is closely related to service branding of companies.

Besides, it is noteworthy that interactions in service brand building involve not only the exchange of operand resources such as physical goods, but also include the exchange of operant resources such as skills and knowledge.

In this book, we propose that the service brand building and value creation of service supply chain model involve interactions between four parties: integrated service providers, customers, players in the supply chain network (also known as micro-specialists or contributors), and society stakeholders (Exhibit 3.3). Society stakeholders have been added as the fourth party in the interactions model because of their importance. Freeman (1984) defined stakeholders as any group or individual who can affect or be affected by the achievement of an organization's objectives. Stakeholders may include those

Exhibit 3.2: Interactions Model to Create Customer Value

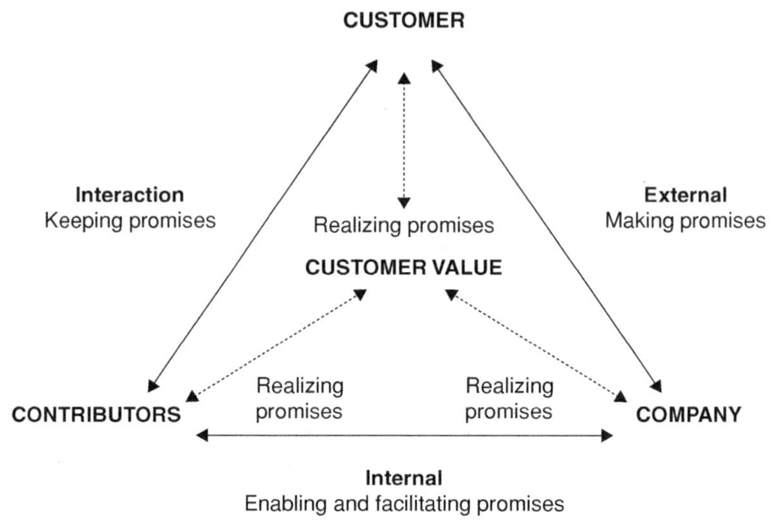

Exhibit 3.3: Service Supply Chain Interactions Model

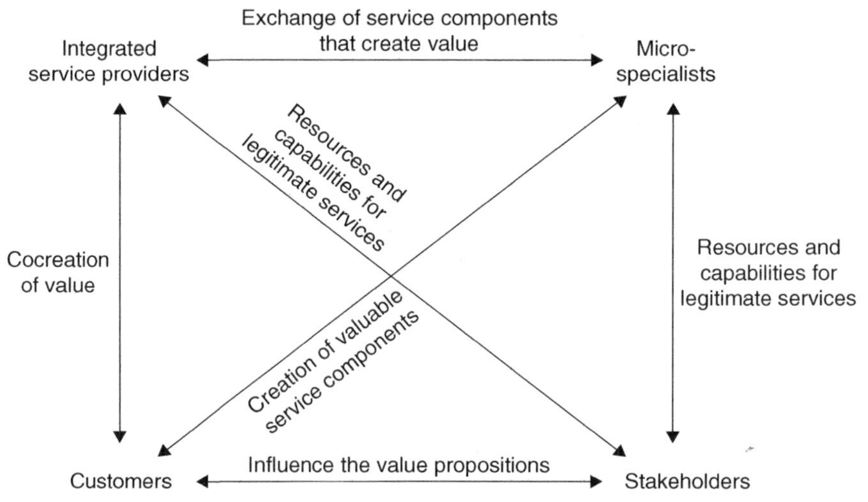

who directly affect the core interests of the company (e.g., customers); those who bring threats or strategic interests to a company (e.g., business partners); and other parties such as shareholders, governments, and communities. Mitchell, Agle, and Woo (1997) suggested that the influence of stakeholders can be determined by three factors—power to influence, legitimacy of their claim, and urgency of their claim. It is a given that a stakeholder has the power to influence another to do a task that others cannot. Suchman (1995) defined legitimacy as a generalized perception or assumption that the actions of an entity are desirable, proper, or appropriate within some socially constructed system of norms, values, and beliefs. Stakeholder urgency includes both criticality and the urgency of their claims that can be reflected in the amount of attention garnered by the claims made.

There are six types of interactions in our interactions model of service supply chain:

Interactions between Integrated Service Provider and Customer

Integrated service providers interact with their customers to cocreate value. As mentioned in Chapter 1, the goal of service-oriented supply chain operations is to achieve customer success, rather than achieving customer satisfaction as in the case of goods-oriented supply chain operations. The interactions go beyond simply meeting a pre-specified set of customer requirements. To achieve customer success, service providers must have a thorough understanding of the operations of its customers, and work to propose new operating solutions for customers so as to realize their full potential to bring future success. On the other hand, customers must not view integrated service providers as mere providers of products or services; instead, they should view integrated service providers as long-term partners who help them gain knowledge and capabilities that they otherwise cannot achieve.

Interactions between Integrated Service Providers and Micro-specialists

Given the complexity of service supply chain operations, it is impossible for a company to complete all tasks by relying on their own efforts and resources. This necessitates the support from micro-specialists. Micro-specialists have strong knowledge and excel in specific service activities. Integrated service providers interact with micro-specialists to unbundle the value chain and exchange with them service components that create value. Based on the understanding of both the customers' requirements and the capability and knowledge of micro-specialists, integrated service providers unbundle the value chains into different elements and outsource the tasks to micro-specialists. To become a core partner of integrated service providers, micro-specialists need to constantly strengthen their capability and knowledge of the particular area and optimize their service processes to create better value.

Interactions between Micro-specialists and Customers

Apart from the interactions between integrated service providers and customers, there may also be an interface for direct interactions between customers and micro-specialists in service supply chain operations. Through specialized operations by micro-specialists, customers enjoy improved efficiency and effectiveness in particular areas; this has laid the foundation for system-wide value creation.

Interactions between Integrated Service Providers and Stakeholders as well as Interactions between Micro-specialists and Stakeholders

During the service supply chain operations, integrated service providers and micro-specialists create value for customers through integration of different resources and capabilities and business model innovations. However, changes initiated by integrated service providers as well as micro-specialists might be seen as nuisances that would hurt the interests of stakeholders such as communities and governments, although they may not necessarily be involved in the actual supply chain operations; therefore, integrated service providers and micro-specialists must constantly communicate with stakeholders to win legitimate status.

Interactions between Stakeholders and Customers

There are always interactions between customers and stakeholders in the same socio-economic network. First, stakeholders indirectly shape the value propositions of customers by influencing the formulations of regulations and policies and their expectations of integrated service providers and micro-specialists. Second, customers also exert their influence on stakeholders by pushing for a more favorable socio-economic environment for their operations.

Case Study: Interactions and Cocreation of Value in Service Supply Chains: Company F in Shangdong

Along with impressive economic growth, people's livelihood in China has shown marked improvements over the years. With a wide variety of products, high operating efficiency, and comfortable shopping environment, supermarkets have become very popular among Chinese consumers and have become a major retail format in urban China. In recent years, this modern retail format is expanding to rural China.

China has a two-tier market structure. Urban-rural disparity has long been a big issue in China. Rural development in China has been lagging behind urban development. Many Chinese farmers have encountered huge difficulties selling their agricultural produce, which hinders income growth. But, rural developments in China are beginning to move in a new direction. To reinvigorate the rural economy, the Chinese government has launched a series of initiatives over the past years, of which, improving the rural retail infrastructure and facilitating rural distribution are high on the agenda. Launched by the Ministry of Commerce (MOFCOM), the Rural Retailing Network Project aims to encourage franchise operations of supermarkets in rural areas. However, many problems have arisen since the launch of the project. Distribution delays, unstable product supply, frequent stock-outs, long ordering cycles, poor inventory turnover, long return cycles, limited product selections, fluctuations in supply prices, and hefty price tags of some products were common problems found in rural procurement and retail distribution. Against this backdrop, some companies in China have actively sought to bring new value to the rural supply chain through service-oriented supply chain management. Company F is an example.

Established in 2003, Company F is a modern logistics company located in Taian city, Shangdong. The company was granted the distribution rights of edible salt in Taian, which is centrally controlled in China. Leveraging on its competitive edge in edible salt distribution, Company F sought to build its network of so-called virtual supermarkets. Today, Company F has six branch companies with 120 employees in China; it has seven modern distribution centers with a distribution fleet of 32 vehicles. The company has total assets worth RMB 77 million. Company F, through third-party logistics arrangements, hopes to facilitate product distribution between the urban communities and the rural markets. It strives to streamline the supply chain and enhance consumers' quality of living by bringing products from manufacturers and farmers directly to retail channels.

Rural Distribution in China: Current Landscape and Problems

China has a large agricultural sector. The rural economy has been pivotal to China's stability and socio-economic developments. In recent years, we witnessed major progress in China's rural developments, such as the launch of supportive initiatives including pilot measures on rural financing reform and the extended coverage of rural pilot insurance scheme. We have also witnessed accelerated improvements in rural infrastructure. Rural incomes are growing at a more satisfactory pace as well—in 2007, the annual per capita income of rural residents reached RMB 4,140, an increase of 15.4% nominally over 2006, or growth of 9.5% year-on-year (yoy). Of these, wage income and income from household business operations were the major growth drivers—an increase of RMB 221 and RMB 224 from those in 2006, respectively. In 2010, the annual per capita income of rural residents reached RMB 5,919, registering an impressive real growth of 10.9% yoy. Unseen in many years, rural income growth exceeded that of the urban residents. Today, many see the rural market as the new growth point in driving consumption in China.

Despite the huge potential, tapping into China's rural market is not an easy task. On one hand, low agricultural productivity remains a major obstacle to boosting income growth. On the other hand, rudimentary retail infrastructure is adding costs to rural distribution; indeed, consumer price indices in rural areas are often higher than those in urban areas. Poor retail infrastructure also makes the rural market a hotbed of poor quality and counterfeit products. According to MOFCOM, in 2006, chain retailers had less than 10% sales share of the overall rural retail market in China. Small-scale mom-and-pop shops and traditional grocery stores dominate the rural retail scene; this poses major challenges for the government authorities in monitoring consumption safety. In fact, China's countryside has suffered the most serious food safety problems. All in all, shopping inconvenience, poor consumption safety, and high distribution costs are major problems of the rural retail landscape in China. As a result, one-third of farmers chose to purchase daily consumerables and other agricultural means of production (seeds, fertilizers, farming tools, etc.) in cities. Besides, the adoption of information technology in rural distribution was also low—only 9.23% of the agricultural wholesale markets in China adopted e-commerce transaction technology.

To bring about an overhaul, the MOFCOM launched the Eleventh Five-Year Plan for the Construction of Rural Market System (hereafter, the "Plan") in 2005. This was the first national plan for the agricultural market. The Rural Retailing Network Project was introduced, with an aim to build a national rural retail network covering 75% of all counties in China by 2010. The MOFCOM also encouraged the development of modern agricultural produce wholesale markets as well as large-scale agricultural produce distribution enterprises in the countryside. In 2005, the MOFCOM and the Ministry of Finance announced financial subsidies and other incentives for enterprises participating in the Rural Retailing Network Project. For instance, enterprises would receive subsidies of RMB 2,000 and RMB 3,000 for opening a retail chain store in a county and in a village, respectively; enterprises could receive an extra RMB 800 subsidy for opening retail stores in the less-developed central and western rural regions.

Different Players of the Rural Supply Chains in China

Developing a modern rural retail network in China requires effective integration and consolidation of different resources to achieve system-wide improvements. There are different major parties involved in China's rural supply chains, including suppliers (manufacturing enterprises), financial institutions, retailers, local governments, and logistics distributors. In addition to sharing different interests and goals, these parties face different challenges as well.

Suppliers

Growing numbers of manufacturing enterprises are keen to sell their products in rural China. However, they have encountered many difficulties that are difficult to tackle by their own efforts. First, the existence of a multi-tier rural distribution system in China means that industrial goods often need to be relayed through regional wholesalers, county-level wholesalers, and township-level wholesalers before being delivered to village stores. Suppliers have weak management control over the long and complicated distribution process. Second, although suppliers can directly manage the regional wholesalers and distributors, they have little knowledge over the operations of lower-tier wholesalers; this makes brand protection and combating counterfeits an uphill battle. Third, suppliers often need to make huge inventory investments in order to effectively penetrate the rural market. That said, the collection of account receivables is often difficult in rural China, compounding the capital strains for many suppliers. Indeed, collecting the account receivables on time and safely is a major concern for many suppliers.

Financial institutions

For many financial institutions, innovations in rural financial services hold the key to the future success of the rural financial market in China. By the end of September 2010, agricultural lending reached RMB 11.13 trillion, accounting for 22.7% of all financial loans in China. However, rural financial services in China remain largely underdeveloped. According to the Ministry of Agriculture, less than 30% of rural households and rural enterprises borrowed from formal channels in 2004. Traditional services such as deposit takings, lending, and remittances account for the bulk of rural financial businesses. On the other hand, businesses such as insurances, third-party payments, and financial consulting are underdeveloped in rural China. Improvements in the legal environment and further policy guidelines have to be in place to boost innovations in rural financial services.

Retailers

Many retailers in China have accelerated rural expansion in recent years. In particular, franchise operations have been growing rapidly. However, there is huge room for improvements in rural retail operations. First, the lack of category management has led to poor product variety and assortments. For instance, in categories such as daily consumerables and household care, rural consumers have few choices and there is a lack of well-known branded products. However, in categories such as food products, the number of brands is overwhelming, though with huge variations in product quality; substandard or counterfeit products are also a big concern. Second, slow inventory turnover has brought huge pressure on retailers' working capital. Third, long order cycles have led to frequent stock-outs and difficult product returns, and this has also hampered sales for products with relatively short shelf life. Fourth, the lack of an advanced information system has resulted in distribution inefficiency.

Local governments

The socialist market economy in China has taken shape after years of market reform. Although the developments in the rural distribution system in China have gained momentum in recent years, the progress in rural areas is still miniscule compared to what has been achieved in the cities. The two-tier market structure and low agricultural productivity in China are major constraints. In view of this, the Chinese government has launched several major policy initiatives including the "Policy Suggestions on Improving Farmers' Income" and "Circular to the Ministry of Commerce on Improving Rural Distribution" by the State Council in 2004, and the "Suggestions on Promoting the New Socialist Countryside" by the State Council in 2006 to improve the livelihood of rural households. The government's initiatives to improve rural distribution revolves around several major themes: (1) promote the development of agricultural logistics, (2) nurture the rural consumption market and improve the rural consumption environment, (3) establish standards for the market of agricultural means of production, and (4) offer policy incentives to encourage farmers to increase participation in rural retail and wholesale trade. These steps are in the right direction; however, given the vast geographical span, effective execution is fraught with challenges and often involves high administrative costs for local governments.

Logistics distributors

Distributing to China's sparsely populated rural areas is costly; therefore, many logistics distributors opt for delivering to rural retail stores through their own central distribution centers, hoping to achieve scale economy. However, many of those distribution centers are manually operated with low levels of mechanization and informatization. Distribution efficiency is poor and logistics costs are high. Many logistics distributors in China earn very slim margins. On the other hand, immature consumption environment and low rural incomes have also hindered logistics development in rural areas. Many farmers in China are highly price-sensitive and there is a large market for lower-priced products, which often come from unscrupulous channels or even counterfeits. This greatly hurts the sales of rural retail stores that procure from regular authorized channels.

Strategy of Company F: Building and Managing a Service-Oriented Rural Supply Chain

Armed with an understanding of the problems of China's rural market and the challenges faced by different rural supply chain players, Company F tries to leverage on its strong network and build a service-oriented rural supply chain, hoping to consolidate the resources and capabilities of different parties and achieve system-wide improvements. Company F believes that no single entity in the rural supply chain can meet this system-wide goal by its own efforts. Therefore, it tries to build a platform to attract different rural supply chain players to contribute to their efforts (Exhibit 3.4). Company F plays a leading role in building and managing the platform, where participants have common interests and work together for a common cause through risks and gain-sharing.

Collaborating with suppliers

Company F established 26 business centers in Taian based on the demographics and geographical characteristics of the city. Each business center provides services to three to four townships and serves two main

Exhibit 3.4: The Basic Interactions Framework of the Service Supply Chain Operations of Company F

functions: helping suppliers deliver their goods from the warehouses of Company F to the rural retail stores and encouraging market developments by inviting rural retail stores to join the business platform, or exploring franchise opportunities. In developing the logistics network, apart from building two logistics centers in Taian, Company F also established second-tier distribution warehouses in areas close to the rural retail stores.

For many suppliers, this "flatter" distribution channel provides a new alternative for a quick product launch across the city. Besides, it also helps protect their interests by eliminating the occurrence of counterfeits.

Moreover, it is a win-win situation for Company F as well. Seeing the huge potential benefits that Company F can bring, suppliers are willing to develop long-term and stable working relationships with Company F. Through securing the supply of branded products at competitive prices, Company F successfully laid a solid foundation for its business.

Collaborating with financial institutions

Company F worked with the Agricultural Bank of China to develop an electronic settlement platform for the project. All participating users (including suppliers, branch companies, business centers, and franchisees) can gain access to this platform. The platform features a "digital wallet" function, which allows revenue from each transaction to be shared and transferred automatically to the accounts of different parties. This greatly helps users reduce their cash cycles and improves cash flows.

Besides, the platform has a mechanism for risk management, and this involves three major initiatives: (1) Company F has the ownership rights to products before they are sold. (2) To avoid non-compliance, franchisees joining the platform must pay 50% of the value of the first batch of products in their franchised stores as collateral. (3) Franchisees also need to pay in advance a certain amount of money, usually the average daily sales revenue, to the Agricultural Bank of China account in order to guarantee that settlements can be made on a timely basis. Settlement efficiency is greatly enhanced. The Agricultural Bank of China, through partnership with Company F, reduces its operating risks and achieves innovations in agricultural financial services.

Collaborating with rural retail store operators

Company F works with two types of rural retail store operators: independent rural retail store operators and franchised store operators under the retail brand "XiaoKanShu." Independent rural retail store operators fully own their stores. Company F does not engage in the direct management of this type of operator and offers only general guidance; and installation of point of sale (POS) system is not required. For independent rural retail store operators, the advantages of working with Company F include getting quality branded products at low prices and enjoying distribution services.

Company F has launched the "XiaoKanShu" franchise business. The franchisees are granted the rights to use the trademark, trade name, and other business resources for which Company F has the license rights, and they carry on business under the uniform business operation system in accordance with the franchise contracts. All franchisees must open an account in a nearby China's Agricultural Bank branch and deposit a certain amount of money as collateral. They also have to install a POS system to share transactions data with Company F on a real-time basis. After deducting the gross profits for franchisees from the daily sales revenue, the money will be deducted directly from the franchisees' account daily. The franchise operations help Company F expand its rural retail network and gain invaluable first-hand knowledge of rural retail operations, which laid a solid foundation for Company F to serve other parties in the service supply chain. For franchised store operators, apart from gaining a stable supply of quality products, they also greatly benefit from the policy supports toward rural retail development.

Collaborating with local governments

Company F regularly communicates with local governments in a bid to gain more policy support for this project. Indeed, local governments believe projects of such nature bring several advantages. First, it alleviates the problem of underutilization of rural facilities. For instance, many of the "XiaoKanShu" stores are retrofitted from previously state-owned factories and residential buildings, and so on, which were no longer in use. Second, it creates rural employment opportunities. Independent rural retail stores hire over 1,600 employees, while the franchisee stores hire more than 16,000 employees (including part-time staff). Third, Company F has offered many training programs to its employees over the years in areas such as modern management and information technology applications; the quality of rural workforce is enhanced. Fourth, it pushes forward the developments of the government project "Rural Information Network Construction" to promote rural informatization. Selected rural retail stores will have computer stations installed with a designated system that allows farmers to gain useful agricultural information online for free. Fifth, consumers' interests are better protected with a better supply of quality products. Sixth, rural retail stores provide a new channel for farmers to sell their products. Seventh, the expansion of this modern retail channel helps reduce government's monitoring costs.

On the other hand, fostering a closer relationship with the government helps Company F enhance its retail branding as well as improve operating performance.

The Results

Leveraging on its successful service-oriented supply chain operations, Company F has built partnerships with a dozen renowned brand companies in China, including Pepsi China, Shangdong Linghua M.S.G Incorporated, Zhejiang Nice Group, Shangdong Taishan Shengliyuan Company, China Sugar Century Company, Wahaha Group, and Colgate-Palmolive (China), and won the regional distribution rights for these products. Its private labels business is also a huge success, and the company is now extending its sales network for its private label products in some bigger cities.

Today, the supermarket business sells its products in eight major categories, including food, beverages, household care, general merchandise, textiles, toys, and alcoholic drinks. Over 200 brands can be found with more than 9,000 stock keeping units (SKUs). With 8 township-level flagship stores, 412 township-level stores, and 8,120 franchised village-level stores in total, Company F achieved sales revenue and gross profit of RMB 160 million and RMB 20.8 million, respectively, in 2006.

Chapter 4

Different Types of Service Supply Chain Strategies: Perspective of Service Providers

To satisfy increasingly diverse customer requirements and succeed in a highly competitive market, more and more manufacturing companies have sought new growth potential in service provisions. Through service supply chain operations and interactions with users, services have become a major source of value creation for many companies. Service supply chain strategies are constantly evolving—the type of service supply chain strategy adopted by companies is a result of adaptations to different customer value propositions as well as changing market environments. What are the different types of service supply chain strategies? How do different types of service supply chains influence service processes? These are all important questions to be answered in service supply chain management.

Different Types of Service Strategies

Service supply chain operations address not only the service elements in supply chains operations and supply chains of service industries but also resource allocation and service integration in response to customer value propositions. Unlike simple exchange relationships as in the general goods market, the inseparability of services is a typical feature of service supply chain operations. This chiefly means that production and consumption are two sides of the same coin in service provision. Service providers interact with their partners as well as customers to create value through services.

Service strategies are diverse and differentiated. Services are classified in different ways. For instance, Jackson and Cooper (1988) differentiated between two types of services procured by manufacturing companies; one type of service is used within the buying company, and the other is passed on to the customers of the buying company. Perhaps the two most well-known classifications of service strategies are the ones by Wynstra, Axelsson, and Van der Valk (2006) and Axelsson and Wynstra (2000, 2002). Wynstra, Axelsson, and Van der Valk (2006) classified four types of services—component services, semi-manufactured services, instrumental services, and consumption services. Component services should be compatible with the final offering of the buying company; they are passed on unaltered to the final customers of the buying company (e.g., maintenance services procured by an equipment manufacturing company). Semi-manufactured services are altered to some extent to integrate them into the buying company's value propositions to its customers (e.g., weather forecasts used by an airline company to chart its flight plans). Instrumental services are used and executed by the buying company with an aim of changing their operations processes (e.g., management consulting services). Consumption services are used within the buying company to support different business processes; consumption services do not affect the core business operations of the buying companies (e.g., gardening services procured by banks). Bjorn and Sweden (2000) shared similar views and put forward four types of services—component services, transformation services, working method services, and consumption services. Component services become part of the offerings of customers without any alterations. Component service providers must have a good understanding of customers' products and how the products are used by the customers' customer. There are two types of components—standard and special components. The usage of a standard component is well-known and, therefore, there is not much need for interactions between customers and specialists. A special component, on the other hand, often involves advanced technology and its usage requires technical expertise and knowledge; there is a stronger need for interactions between customers and specialists. Transformation services are characterized by modifications by the buying company before delivering to the customer's customer; transformation service provisions require deep understanding among service providers, customers, and customers' customers. Working method services strongly affect the manufacturing and operations of customers. With the change in the way of working, it is essential that the working method fits in well with customers' operations. Finally, the definition of consumption services is largely the same as the one by Wynstra, Axelsson, and Van der Valk (2006). Consumption services are used within the buying company without them becoming part of the company's final product.

The above classifications touch upon the requirements of interactions between service providers, buying companies, and end customers. However, not much attention has been paid to the driving factors behind different types of services. Let us now investigate the driving forces behind different service strategies.

Driving Factors behind Different Service Strategies

The organization of service supply chains are determined by a multitude of internal and external factors. Lewin, Weigelt, and Emery (2003) classified three types of adaptation and selection strategies by companies. The first strategy is concerned with company-level capabilities and strategies; the second is concerned with the technical environment, that is, adaptation to the industry characteristics and environment; and the third is concerned with adaptation to the macro- and institutional environment. The adaptation and selection strategies have a direct impact on the service supply chain operations risks and the corresponding organization methods and structures.

In terms of internal factors, the resources and capability of service providers are key for them to win and sustain a competitive edge. Day (1994) distinguished two types of capabilities: inside-out and outside-in. Inside-out capabilities focus on a company's internal resources and capabilities that help it respond effectively to market demand; some examples include manufacturing, logistics and transportation, and resources allocation. Outside-in capabilities are the skills and competencies of a company that help it grasp and forecast changes in market (market sensing capabilities such as market research) and operate more effectively than its competitors in the marketplace (market bonding capabilities such as customer relationship management). On this basis, Song, Chatterjee, and Jingliang (2011) further advanced the capability framework for service supply chain operators and suggested that resources/supply capability, demand management capability, and strategic fit with downstream players are three critical factors to competitiveness.

Meanwhile, external factors are related to issues that are raised in the technical and institutional environment of a company (Oliver 1997). The technical environment refers to the characteristics of an industry that companies operate within. Companies strive to maximize profits under these industry situations—companies in industries with high market concentration tend to enjoy more resources to carry out technology progress and innovation activities, while those in industries with lower market concentration tend to share fewer resources, and often seek to expand market influence through vertical and horizontal integration (Scott 1989). The characteristics of industries are major determinants of the service types of companies. According to the structure-conduct-performance approach in industrial organization theory, the structure of an industry determines the conduct of companies, and the conduct of the companies determines an industry's performance (Bain 1956). According to Shamsie (2003), elements of an industry structure include economies of scale, barriers to market entry, diversification, product differentiation, market concentration, and so on. On the other hand, institutional factors place emphasis on gaining legitimacy by conforming to rules and belief systems prevailing in an environment. Apart from the regulative and legal legitimacy, companies must win the support of their stakeholders (Suchman 1995). The institutional theory suggests that there are three pillars of legitimacy: regulative, normative, and cultural-cognitive. Regulative legitimacy is earned by conforming to legal rules and regulations. Normative legitimacy is earned by conforming to norms or values that are expected as social obligations. Cultural-cognitive legitimacy is gained by conforming to the shared understanding that the institution requests its members to follow (Scott 2001).

Companies operate with a goal to maximize profits using their own resources. At the same time, their external environment is bound to influence the operating activities of companies. Companies are constrained by their own resources and capabilities, as well as different industry and institutional characteristics. Jüttner, Peck, and Christopher (2003) considered risks to include external risks such as political risks, market risks, uncertainties in consumer demand, as well as those caused by human errors such as operational risks, customer risks, and cooperation risks. Thus, we can see that supply chain risks vary for different companies. Often, the higher the supply chain risks, the higher the management costs. Correspondingly, transaction costs can be seen as the price for bounded rationality, asymmetric market information, and market uncertainties. Williamson (2002) pointed out that factors such as information asymmetry, opportunistic behavior, and market uncertainties during interactions between companies and external parties incur transaction costs. Service providers adopt different service structures and provision models to lower management and transaction costs.

Generally speaking, in industries with lower entry thresholds and those less impacted by institutional factors, customers tend to pay stronger attention to economic benefits. Meanwhile, in industries where entry thresholds are high and influences of institutional factors are strong, customers tend to place stronger emphasis on sustainable development and business innovations.

To summarise, three fundamental factors: (1) resources and capabilities, (2) industry characteristics, and (3) institutional characteristics determine the types of supply chain risks and the revenue targets of the supply chain, and thereby impact the service structure and interactions, which finally affect the service supply chain performance (Exhibit 4.1).

Exhibit 4.1: Factors Affecting the Service Supply Chain Performance

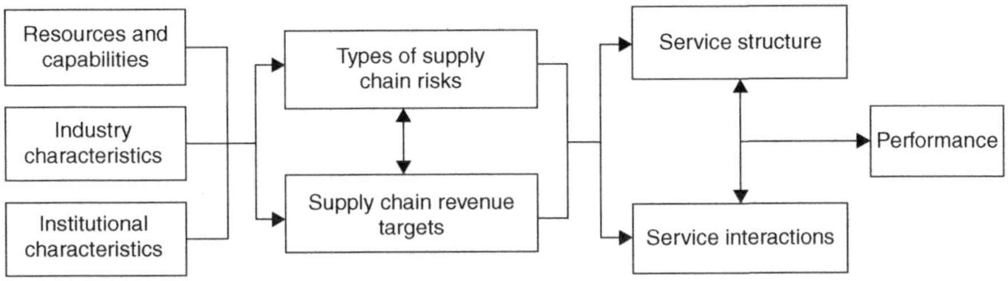

To illustrate how different dynamic forces shape service supply chain structures, we will study the case of four companies in China. We will begin with the company background, and then explore how internal and external factors such as resources, industry characteristics, and institutional factors shape the service supply chain strategies of companies. Finally, we will discuss the results of implementing the service supply chain strategies. We collect company information using different methods, including company visits, in-depth interviews, industry research reports and development plans, and company annual reports.

Case study: Service Supply Chain Model Featuring Embedded Services in Products—The Service Supply Chain of Company W[1]

For a service supply chain model that features embedded services in products, services are consumed alongside material products. Furthermore, value is created during the process.

[1] Information and statistics of this case study are collected from field visits, company interviews, and the case studies database of the Business Faculty of Renmin University, China.

Company Background

Established in 1993, Company W is a high-end hotel detergent manufacturer headquartered in Beijing. Its 24,000 square metre (sq. m) production base is located in the Industrial Development Zone in Tongzhou District, Beijing. With a factory area of 12,000 sq. m, Company W has an annual production capacity of 15,000 tons of different types of fine chemical products. The total employee strength of Company W increased from 18 in 1993 to over 300 in 2001. Company W has grown from a small regional company to a national company with 17 branch offices and 2 production bases in China. The product line of Company W includes kitchen detergents, laundry detergents, industrial collection, commercial dishwashers, and so on.

Industry Analysis

The commercial detergents production industry in China has rapidly expanded in sync with the stellar growth of the catering and tourism industries since the 1990s. The production of commercial detergents does not require high technological inputs; however, the formula and target users of commercial detergents are totally different from those of detergents for home use. Commercial detergents have a chemical formula that brings about stronger cleansing action, and they must be used together with other specialized appliances. The target customers of commercial detergents include hotels, restaurants, office buildings, hospitals, commercial laundries, food and beverage manufacturers, and so on. Take the example of star-rated hotels that use a wide range of detergents. Several types of professional detergents are used for housekeeping and cleansing in public areas, kitchens, laundries, and so on.

In fact, the use of commercial detergents was first introduced by foreign hotel operators in China in the mid-1980s. In 1986, Diversey, a provider of commercial cleaning, sanitation, and hygiene solutions based in the United States established a joint venture with Dalian Chemical Company Limited to form China's first company specializing in commercial detergent production. In the 1990s, the market became more mature and we witnessed a number of solely owned and private small-scale joint ventures enter the market.

The commercial detergent market in China can be divided into three segments: (1) US-based Ecolab and SC Johnson, offering premium product and services quality, are the two players in the high-end market. Ecolab and SC Johnson products have long been used by many companies and they enjoy strong brand reputation in the international market. In the hotel commercial detergents market alone, the two companies achieved sales revenue of RMB 150 million. (2) Over 20 domestic manufacturers compete in the mid-range segment. They offer good-quality products and services at more affordable prices. However, these companies are largely homogenous in products, promotions, and other various aspects. (3) Over 1,000 smaller local companies compete in the low-price segment. These companies usually target specific regional markets and have grabbed a certain share of market with low prices and strong local connections. However, product and service quality of these companies vary a lot.

With the rise in incomes, the spending habits of Chinese consumers have also changed. Increased spending on travel and catering has encouraged sales of commercial detergents. For instance, for 100 standard rooms in a star-rated hotel, the expense on detergents would cost RMB 200,000. Star-rated hotels in China have a total of 1.5 standard rooms; the size of hotel-use commercial detergent market is estimated to be around RMB 3 billion. If we also include hospitals, office buildings, commercial laundries, restaurants, and so on, the market demand could exceed RMB 5 billion.

Despite huge potential, the commercial detergent market is highly competitive. First, looking at the industry characteristics, a large number of small- and medium-sized commercial detergent companies are poorly differentiated. Their products are highly similar in variety, packaging, and even names; however, there are vast differences in product quality. This negatively impacts the competing environment, which is reflected in the following factors:

1. **Homogenous competition**
The entry threshold for commercial detergent market is low due to limited technological content in production. Whenever a new product is launched by a company, the market gets flooded with many copycat lower-priced products.

2. **Difficulties in account receivable collection**
Restaurants and hotels mostly pay for the commercial detergents they procure after product delivery. The common payment periods are usually over two or three months, and some even over six months, resulting in the tie-up of suppliers' capital.

3. **Heavy product damage and depreciation**
Due to much stronger market power and loopholes in the payment methods, buyers often procure detergent products in a large batch; however, they do not pay much attention to the storage conditions (e.g., temperature and humidity) and the usage registration system. Often, when these result in product damages, buyers simply ask for product returns claiming that there are quality problems.

4. **Small-scale commercial detergents manufacturers**
To enter the highly regionalized markets in China, local connections as well as sales and marketing efforts are necessary for success. Kickbacks are very common in this poorly regulated market.

Second, in terms of market demand for resources and capabilities, there are huge obstacles that are difficult to overcome in both commercial detergent and commercial dishwasher markets. In the commercial detergent market, manufacturers would generally adopt the "guarantee cost" operations model when dealing with hotels and restaurants operators with good reputation and cost control record. This model guarantees that the monthly expense on commercial detergents of the operators stay within a fixed range. There are several benefits of this model: (1) Hotels can keep zero detergents inventory. Hotel operators can pay for the detergents after use, which greatly helps reduce capital tie-ups. (2) Final expenses on detergents are charged according to actual hotel occupancy. Hotel operators and detergents suppliers would deliberate beforehand the standard cleansing expense for usage in each room and use this standard rate to calculate the expense on detergents afterward based on actual occupancy. Most hotel operators prefer to adopt the guarantee cost model; however, it is associated with many practical problems. First, commercial detergent suppliers do not know the actual hotel occupancy. Second, many hotel laundries also serve external customers; it is difficult to calculate the volume of detergents used in hotel rooms. Third, detergent usage is much higher in some hotel areas such as fitness centers than in an average hotel room. Therefore, most commercial detergent manufacturers have concerns over potential losses due to miscalculations regarding the use of detergents.

As for the commercial dishwasher market, the use of commercial dishwasher is only popular in three-star or higher rated hotels. Driven by a strong desire to save costs due to intensive price competition, many catering enterprises in China prefer manual dishwashing, although hygiene is less guaranteed and tableware damage (10% per month) is 10 times higher than when using dishwashers. Catering enterprises are reluctant to use commercial dishwashers because of the extra expenses needed on special detergents, accessory change, maintenance costs, and so on.

The Service Supply Chain Strategy of Company W

Company W hoped to seek new breakthroughs in its service supply chain by working to develop a new kind of automatic detergent dispenser for dishwashers, with an aim to reduce the human element in detergent usage and change user behavior. The principle of detergent dispenser in dishwashers is to automatically detect and adjust the concentration of detergent in the dishwasher tank. Using automatic dispensers can minimize human factors in detergent usage and bring about a more stable cleaning performance.

However, all automatic detergent dispensers in the market then were imported and designed for powder detergent use only. And, powder detergents have a major disadvantage—they tend to absorb moisture and can easily become caked or lumpy, thereby affecting the accuracy of dispensers. Automatic dispensers were also expensive. Back then, only a few manufacturers in the world made automatic dispensers, and replacement accessories could not always be easily found.

After evaluating both customer needs and resources and in-house capability, Company W expended large research and development (R&D) efforts on dishwasher-making technology. The efforts paid off. Finally, Company W launched its own dishwashers featuring its proprietary automatic liquid detergent dispensers. It managed to resolve all previous problems of powder dispensers, and its ground-breaking technology and innovative dishwashers received wide acceptance soon after the launch.

Company W also introduced eight different proprietary commercial liquid laundry detergents after the launch of dishwashers, including chlorine bleach, oxygen bleach, softener, neutralizer, sizing agent, and three different types of laundry detergents that must be used with automatic laundry dispensers developed by Company W. The automatic laundry dispensers developed by Company W include 99 preset functions, such as towel wash and bed linen wash; they can automatically discharge the right type and amount of detergent during various washing stages according to the wash loads and the functions set. The liquid laundry detergent collections solve the old problem of unstable washing performance due to human factors and help Company W differentiate from the rest of the market. As customers must simultaneously use the detergents and automatic detergent dispensers by Company W to enjoy the benefits, this creates very good technical conditions for the company to draw customers.

The automatic laundry dispensers by Company W also have the "load statistics" function that connects with the computer system in the laundry; laundry operators can therefore, fully grasp the wash load each day. In this way, a new pricing model came into effect that charges hotel operators based on the exact wash load. There are a number of benefits of adopting the new pricing model:

1. Better cleaning performance

Discharge of detergent according to the preset functions and wash load reduces the human element in operations, giving better and stable cleaning performance. Increasing automation and standardization of laundry operations also help hotel laundries expand their external business.

2. Low requirements on laundry operators
Company W developed the dispenser and its preset washing functions after inspecting actual commercial laundry operations (e.g., facilities and water supply); the dispensers are easy-to-use and do not require technical knowledge. This helps hotel operators lower staff costs.

3. Accurate statistics on detergent use
This saves a great amount of time and efforts in price negotiations and auditing the actual use of detergents, and significantly reduces disputes and conflicts between detergent suppliers and their customers. Customer relationship management costs are also lowered.

As for the commercial dishwasher market, prior to 2007, Company W treated commercial dishwashers and commercial dishwasher detergents businesses as two independent streams. As China's catering market continues to grow and people pay more attention to hygiene standards, more and more catering enterprises are under increasing pressure to use dishwashers. That said, unlike many other countries, there are no compulsory regulations in China stating that catering enterprises must use dishwashers; therefore, most catering enterprises adopt a wait-and-watch attitude toward adopting dishwashers.

After a detailed market study, Company W launched a new dishwasher leasing business model. The key idea of this model is to offer all-in-one solutions to catering enterprises. Paying only a fixed monthly lease fee, catering enterprises can enjoy both the benefits of the "Winchem" brand dishwasher and detergents. Instead of having at least three suppliers for dishwashers, maintenance, and commercial detergents, Company W can serve all the cleaning needs for catering enterprises, which improves convenience levels and brings huge cost reductions. By adopting the leasing model, catering enterprises do not have to invest huge sums of money to purchase commercial dishwashers, and do not need to spend further on detergents as well as dishwasher maintenance.

Let us use Little Sheep, one of China's biggest restaurant chains, as an example. In 2009, Little Sheep had a total of 445 restaurants in China; of these, 166 restaurants were directly owned and 279 restaurants were franchised. Given the large kitchen area and huge customer traffic, conveyor type dishwashers would be preferable. If Little Sheep were to purchase one conveyor type dishwasher for each restaurant, it would cost the chain at least RMB 22.3 million. Besides, the chain needs to spend big sums of money on maintenance and detergent.

Exhibit 4.2 illustrates the differences in purchasing and leasing commercial dishwashers.

Exhibit 4.2: Purchasing vs. Leasing Commercial Dishwashers

Purchasing commercial dishwashers	Leasing commercial dishwashers
Asset ownership	No asset ownership
Depreciation over use	Not Applicable
Good cleaning performance	Good cleaning performance
One-year warranty	Permanent warranty
High expenses on detergents	Included in the fixed lease fee
Expenses on maintenance, services, and accessories	Exempt from the expenses on maintenance, services, and accessories
Waiting time for maintenance cannot be guaranteed	Quick maintenance response

Exhibit 4.3 compares the effectiveness of manual dishwashing and mechanical dishwashing. Mechanical dishwashing has a distinct edge.

Exhibit 4.3: Effectiveness of Manual Dishwashing vs. Mechanical Dishwashing

Manual dishwashing	Mechanical dishwashing
Difficult to standardize hygiene requirements	Standardized hygiene requirements
High labor costs	Low labor costs
Heavy labor work	Less labor work
Heavy use of water	Little use of water
No electricity expense	Electricity expense
High damage rate of tableware	Low damage rate of tableware
Poor working conditions	Good working conditions
Inconsistent cleaning performance	Consistent cleaning performance

For a long time, the catering enterprise market segment was deemed stagnant for many dishwasher manufacturing companies. However, the lease model changed the prevalent picture and has quickly won acceptance from customers since its launch. Apart from star-rated hotels, the customer base of Company W was successfully extended to include a large number of catering enterprises in China.

Characteristics of Service Supply Chains and Performance of Company W

The service supply chain strategy has greatly enhanced the performance of Company W. It registered improvements in both revenue and profits. In 2009, its revenue grew to RMB 98.3 million; Company W rose to become the number three player in the industry. Products of Company W have become more competitive. For instance, in Beijing, dishwashers' penetration of the market jumped from 132 to 778 sets in just one year. After the launch of automatic detergent dispensers, the annual revenue of Company W climbed from several million in 2007 to RMB 20 million in 2009. For a long time, the profit margin has been lower than 10% in the commercial dishwasher market, largely due to heavy price competition in the traditional product sales model. By bundling the use of products and services, Company W saw its net profit margin rise to around 30% after the launch of the lease model. Besides, it has also successfully nurtured long-term partnerships with many of its customers.

As discussed, many target customers of Company W are highly price-sensitive. Therefore, when redesigning its service supply chain, Company W uses a single product (liquid detergent dispenser or commercial dishwasher) as a starting point to change customers' operation process and their perceptions toward product pricing. Customers are relieved from the burden of purchase decision-making, quality control, and other relevant operating and management costs, both direct and indirect. This is particularly true in the commercial dishwasher market. Embedding a range of services in the products has helped Company W depart from the traditional model that separates sales of products and services; through different complementary products and services, Company W enjoys economic and strategic benefits. This type of service supply chain is a typical model featuring embedded services in a product (Exhibit 4.4).

Products with embedded services differ from traditional products in many ways. First of all, design and innovations of traditional products tend to emphasize use value and differentiation in use value; however, the design and innovation of products featuring embedded services are different—internalizing services is the prime focus. Through product purchases, customers also enjoy services alongside the use value of products. As in our previous examples of liquid detergent dispenser and commercial

Exhibit 4.4: Service Supply Chain Model Featuring Embedded Services in a Product

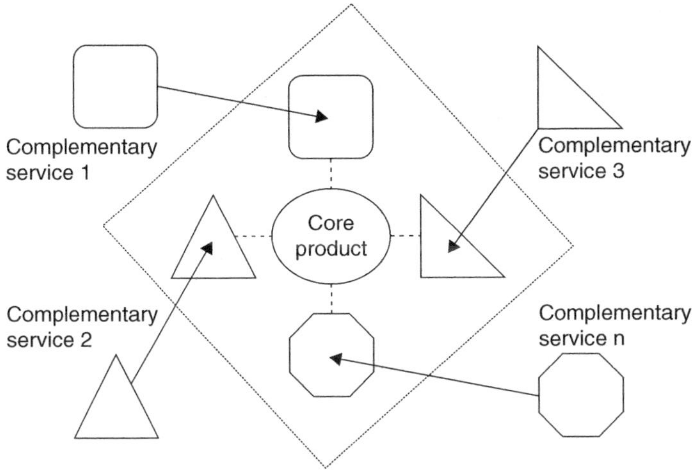

dishwasher, the core focus is not the direct use value of the products, but on achieving a new operations model through these products so that customers can enjoy service gains with lower integrated costs. Besides, the delivery process is different. For traditional products, once the product is handed to the customers, delivery is completed. However, for products with embedded services, delivery remains unfinished even after the products reach the customers. Third, providers play a different role. Providers of traditional products are simply product suppliers or manufacturers. However, to offer products with embedded services, providers must also be the designers and component integrators of the service systems.

Case Study: Service Supply Chain Model Featuring Seamless Connections of Different Supply Chain Players—The Service Supply Chain of Company H

The concept of seamless connections in service supply chain has been borrowed from the information technology industry. In the context of service supply chain, seamless connections means connecting different supply chain partners and integrating their resources and capabilities through establishing agreements so as to create value for the customers as well as to reduce the transaction costs previously hiked up by decentralized management and scattered resources.

Company Background

Established in early 2005, Company H is a multinational investment management company located in Shenzhen, Guangdong. It mainly offers global standard integrated supply chain services to large-scale international manufacturers invested in China. Company H has 12 fully-owned and joint-venture branch companies in China, Hong Kong, Japan, Australia, and Canada, offering international trade, import and export logistics, information system development, management consulting, and back-end support services. Company H has built vendor-managed inventory (VMI) logistics centers for many international manufacturers; its just-in-time (JIT) E-Kanban distribution model has successfully lowered inventories for many manufacturers. Besides, Company H facilitates customs clearance and offers door-to-door services across different countries. The company has formed strategic alliances with international logistics giants such as Hitachi Transport System from Japan, Rhenus Logistics from Germany, and VISA Global Logistics from Australia; the strong global network has helped lay a solid foundation for Company H to offer global supply chain services. Company H provides strategic planning to international companies in China and can manage the non-core business operations for them. In 2005, Company H won the "No. 25 in China Logistics Top 100s" and the "4A class integrated logistics services provider in China" awards.

Industry Analysis of the Electric Lighting Industry in China

With major advancement in technology, the electric lighting industry in China has registered impressive growth in the past decade. Today, China is the global manufacturing center of the industry. In 2010, the annual output of electric light bulbs approximated 18.7 billion, and the total output value exceeded RMB 72 billion. The total asset value of the industry reached RMB 48.3 billion in 2010, up by 28% year-on-year (yoy). Competition in the electric lighting industry is intensifying. Many existing players are accelerating their expansion in China, and at the same time, a large number of foreign players are rushing to the market. In 2010, there were 931 registered electric lighting enterprises in China, up by 16% yoy. Most of the domestic enterprises are located in coastal provinces and municipalities such as Guangdong, Jiangsu, Shanghai, Zhejiang, and Fujian.

However, in terms of overall production performance, China's electric lighting industry is still lagging behind its foreign counterparts. On one hand, the quality of the production materials is relatively poor, for example, (1) the dual filament bulb used for general lighting has low luminous efficacy; (2) there is low production of filaments with fuse, and they are of variable quality; (3) lead-free tubes used in environmental lighting and water-based fluorescent paint used in fluorescent lighting are not produced in China; (4) production of nano-sized high-purity aluminum oxides, adhesives, dispersants, and deformers cannot meet domestic demand; (5) mercury-based fluorescent technology is underdeveloped; and (6) increase in production and further improvements in the quality of mercury, sodium, and metal halide bulb shells are needed. On the other hand, there is further room for improvement in the level of automation to improve quality control. Currently, we see a need for major research and development in the production line technology of T8, T5, and compact fluorescent lights.

Reducing energy consumption is of utmost importance to China. In China's Eleventh Five-year Plan Period, China launched and revised a series of environmental protection laws and regulations, such as "The Law of the People's Republic of China on Energy Conservation, Law of the People's Republic of China on the Prevention and Control of Water Pollution," and the "Renewable Energy Law of the People's Republic of China." Relevant authorities have also put forward important documents such as the "Circular on Carrying out Key Works for Establishing Resources-saving Society (2005)," the "Decision about Strengthening Energy Saving Work from the State Council (2006)," and the "Opinions on Accelerating the Closure of Small Thermal Power Generation Units (2007)." The government also launched a series of supportive measures to promote energy conservation in China's electricity industry. It implemented a new target responsibility and accountability system for energy conservation and strengthened monitoring and the energy conservation performance of local governments and electricity enterprises (including pollutant reduction of top five electricity enterprises in every province and city) would be made public every year. China's Twelfth Five-year Plan has put forward specific energy conversation goals with a number of important quantitative indicators that are rigid and compulsory. China strives to reduce its reliance on coal to produce electricity in the future. Non-fossil sources such as water, nuclear, wind, and solar energy accounted for 8.3% of China's total primary energy use in 2010; it is stated in the plan that as a share of total primary energy, non-fossil energy should reach 11.4% by 2015, and 15% by 2020. Besides, China is committed to reduce its carbon intensity (the amount of carbon emitted for each unit of GDP) by 17% from 2011 to 2015. All in all, the Chinese government is keen to adjust the country's energy structure and has adopted a wide range of taxation, financial, and legal initiatives to push forward energy conversation. This has profound implications for different industries in China. Local governments have been prompted to shift their attention to energy conversation targets, instead of solely focusing on the amount of fixed asset investments of projects.

On the other hand, in terms of capacity requirements, energy conservation remains a huge challenge for most manufacturing companies in China. In the past year, two-thirds of Chinese provinces experienced different levels of electricity blackouts, and some even introduced restrictions on power use to curb demand. However, energy consumption in the country continues to increase rapidly. For example, the electricity use in lighting showed a rapid increase in the past two years. It is estimated that lighting accounts for 10%–12% of total electricity use in China. Many lighting products used in China today are energy-inefficient. Indeed, the market of energy-saving lighting products has huge potential. Currently, over 80% of lighting products in China use the T8 light technology; nearly all supermarkets, hospitals, factories, offices, and schools use T8 lighting products. However, today, the new generation of T5 light technology can achieve energy savings with better performance over T8 light technology, in terms of glare, average life, and stability. Replacing T8 with T5 lighting products can bring energy savings in three major ways: (1) electrical ballasts in T5 lighting products have higher lumens-per-watt efficiency and can save energy by 20%; (2) T5 light tubes use three-wavelength fluorescent powder, which offer higher lighting efficiency than T8 light tubes that use halogen powder, thus reduces energy usage by 16%; and (3) some T5 light tubes have a reflector installation that fully utilizes light sources from different directions, thus lowering energy usage by 15%. Overall, converting from T8 lights to T5 lights with electronic ballasts yields energy savings of 30%–40%, and from T8 lights with inductive ballasts yields energy savings of 40%–50%. However, there is a major issue in promoting the use of T5 lighting products. Despite substantial energy savings, T5 lighting products are much more expensive than other lighting products in the market. If customers are to adopt T5 lighting products, they have to pay a huge one-off cost—they must purchase a new grille lamp tray for T5 lighting products, and each T5 lighting product (3–40 watts) costs around RMB 400. It would easily cost companies millions to replace all lighting products, adding to their financial burdens.

Service Supply Chain Strategy of Company H

In view of this, Company H proposed a range of "seamless connection" services hoping to lower the costs for customers converting to T5 lighting (Exhibit 4.5).

Exhibit 4.5: Company H's Seamless Connection Service Model

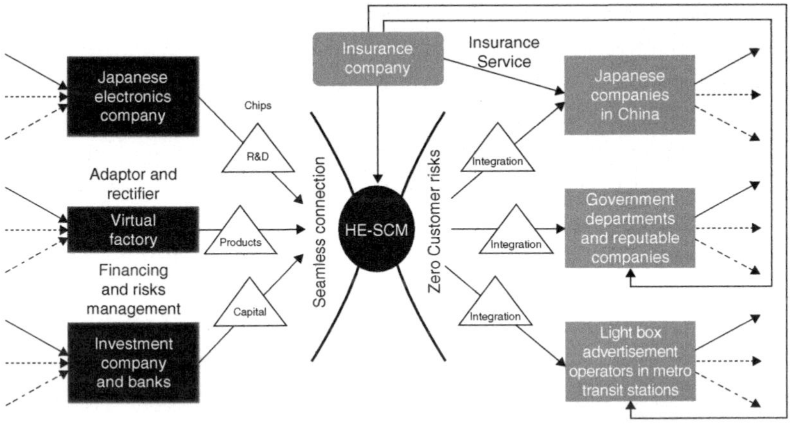

Company H helped solve the conversion problem encountered by customers on the technical front by designing and manufacturing adaptors compatible with both T5 and T8 technology. Customers can place a T5 light tube directly on to the adaptor, and install it on the original T8 lamp. However, customers cannot achieve energy savings in this manner. To solve this problem, Company H collaborated with a Japanese electronics company to develop a new type of rectifier. Using both a rectifier and an adaptor, customers can achieve energy savings.

The driving force behind Company H's launch of the adaptor and rectifier, however, was not the new income from manufacturing, retail, and distribution. Instead, Company H eyed the opportunity to develop a seamlessly connected electric lighting supply chain on this basis. Company H made great efforts to minimize risks faced by different players along the service supply chain.

First, to address customers' concerns on heavy upfront costs, Company H put forward a "zero-risk" customer-experience approach, that is, customers could outsource their lighting needs to Company H without incurring any expenses, and Company H would then invest in retrofitting the lighting system as well as the T5 lighting products of the customers. Generally speaking, both sides would sign a three-year contract, which states the proportion of gain-sharing from reduction in electricity use. Customers bore zero risks as they would not need to pay any money if the goal of electricity savings was not reached.

Second, despite potential energy savings, many customers were concerned that outsourcing lighting needs might cause interruptions in their core manufacturing operations. To safeguard customers' interests, Company H formed a strategic partnership with an insurance company. Customers would be covered for any losses from production disruptions due to the service problems of Company H.

Third, to effectively realize low-cost upstream operations, Company H did not invest in building new factories for the manufacturing of adaptors and rectifiers. Instead, it collaborated with an electronic import and export trading company. A legal transfer agreement was signed between both parties—Company H would have the registered ownership rights to the production lines, which the trading company would contribute to the fixed asset investments, and Company H would contribute to the production technology and management; both sides would share the revenue derived from the manufacturing operations. As for the source of capital, Company H established a new investment company for the project and injected capital; it also worked with banks in some regions to support the operations of its service supply chain.

Lastly, as Company H had to make huge prepayments to its customers on T5 technology conversion, it was very cautious in selecting its target customers. To lower its risks, customers' company reputation, business performance, and willingness to build long-term and stable relationships were key considerations. Company H targeted the following three types of customers: (1) the Top 500 Japanese companies in China, such as Fuji Xerox, YKK, and Omron; (2) reputable companies and government departments in China; and (3) light box advertisement operators in metro transit stations in some big cities in China.

By aligning the interests of different service supply chain members with the "contract energy management (EMC) + supply chain + financing" operating model, Company H managed to successfully lower the electricity expenses of its customers and solve the high costs associated with T5 technology conversion.

The Results

The "seamless connection" supply chain services of Company H helped it develop win-win relationships with its customers. Company H was able to draw dozens of new customers every year. Besides, the new operating model brought huge benefits to the customers of Company H. For instance, one of its manufacturing customers originally used 5,000 T8 fluorescent light tubes (40W) for its plants. Based on an average of 12 hours use per day, electricity expense was RMB 864,000 per year. After the conversion to 5,000 T5 LED light tubes (15W), based on the same energy usage rate, the annual electricity expense dropped to RMB 345,600, resulting in an impressive savings of RMB 520,000.

Customers of Company H enjoy energy savings without any increase in costs. Company H made use of electric lighting products as a starting point, and moved along the service supply chain, from product manufacturing through installation to different services, to integrate different physical, information, and capital flows. Highly effective integration of different processes and components lowers operations costs. This is a model of a seamlessly connected service supply chain (Exhibit 4.6).

Exhibit 4.6: The Seamlessly Connected Service Supply Chain of Company H

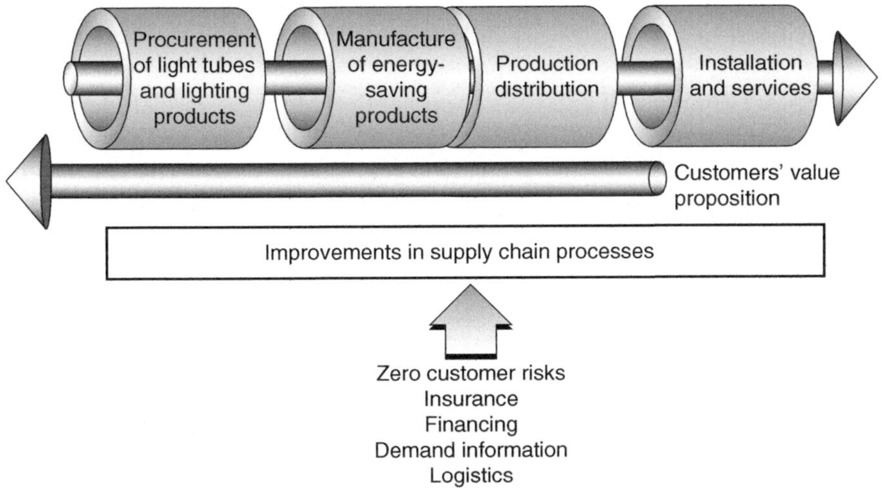

Case Study: Service Supply Chain Model Featuring Business Processes Integration—The Service Supply Chain of Company B

A service supply chain model featuring business processes integration focuses on industry operations processes and seeks to integrate different resources to lower costs and achieve greater value for customers by offering total solutions. The "packaged" products and services can boost customer loyalty and increase contract renewal rates.

Company Background

Company B is a turbo-machinery manufacturer; its mother company was founded in 1968. The mother company started production in 1975 and had been under the direct management of the Ministry of Machine Building Industry and the ShaanXi Mechanical Industry Bureau; later in 1985, the Xian government assumed responsibility of the management of the mother company. In 1999, Company B was founded. In 2009, Company B had a total of 2,969 employees and a total asset value of RMB 3.31 billion. Company B mainly manufactured five types of machines: axial compressors, top pressure recovery turbines, centrifugal compressors, centrifugal blowers, and ventilating machines (Exhibit 4.7). With a total of 80 collections, Company B manufactures over 2,000 products with different specifications. Company B mainly caters to customers in the fields of steel, metallurgy, and petrochemical industries. Axial compressors and top pressure recovery turbines featuring high efficiency, energy saving, and low environmental impact are the key products of Company B; and the key competitors in the area include reputable international players such as MANturbo from Germany, and Siemens and Mitsui from Japan. Company B has won the Second Class Prize for Science and Technology Progress as well as the "China Top Brand" for these two key products. Company B has obtained certifications for international standards, environmental protection, as well as industrial health and safety management.

Exhibit 4.7: Five Major Types of Products of Company B

Axial compressors

Top pressure recovery turbines

Centrifugal compressors

Centrifugal blowers

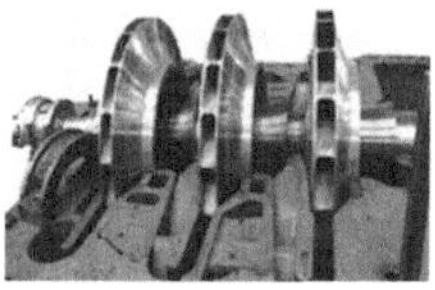

Ventilating machines

Since its establishment, Company B has undergone four phases of developments.

1. First phase: Manufacturing of traditional blowers (1980–2000)
During this period, Company B was one of the most important players in China, manufacturing centrifugal blowers and axial compressors. Machine manufacturing was the only business of Company B. It mainly relied on adopting foreign technology, adding new facilities and workers, and selling self-manufactured machinery to drive growth. Typically, Company B adopted a traditional operational model that relied heavily on scale expansion. In 2000, Company B had 3,326 employees, and its total output value and profit were RMB 340 million and RMB 14 million, respectively. Company B derived all of its profits from machinery sales.

During this period, Company B successfully built its own R&D capability in turbine technology. In fact, in the early 1980s, Company B faced multiple problems of aging facilities, low production technology, and poor product offerings; to tackle these problems, its management was determined to nurture its own R&D capability, and the company had collaborated with different universities and research institutes such as the Xi'an Jiaotong University and the Chinese Academy of Sciences to develop new products. On the other hand, it accelerated the pace of introducing foreign technology, such as the introduction of state-of-the-art axial compressor production technology from Switzerland, to facilitate assimilation of new ideas. In 1998, Company B became the only company in China with the capability to design and manufacture axial compressors.

Through the assimilation of new ideas and innovations, Company B extended its business from metallurgy to also include oil refining, fertilizers, pharmaceuticals, electricity, wind tunnel testing, sewage treatment, and the CCPP industries. Between 1986 and 2000, Company B had invested a total of RMB 157 million on technology upgrade and the purchase of computer numerical control (CNC) equipment; it has built the country's largest and most advanced testing station and technology center of the blower industry.

2. Second phase: The "two transformations" (2000)
The year 2000 was the turning point for both the strategy and operations of Company B. Company B had a major breakthrough in its operations philosophy. Company B recognized major disadvantages in the traditional manufacturing model, which relied on introducing new technology, adding new facilities and workers, and sales of self-manufactured products to drive growth; however, companies often face fierce competition as the products they launched could be easily replicated by competitors. Operating risks are high and profit margins are slim. Besides, manufacturing facilities require heavy investment;

the investment payback periods are long. Thus, Company B strived to climb the value ladder by strengthening services and branding, while maintaining its edge in facilities and technology.

Company B put forward the "two transformations" strategy. The first transformation highlighted a customer-driven business model, wherein Company B would investigate customer demand carefully and offer solutions to customers based on their needs. It aimed, on one hand, to increase profits by offering more added value, and on the other hand, to improve profit margins through systematic procurement with suppliers. The second transformation focused on branding. The rationale being that operations focus should go beyond physical products and facilities; instead, intangible assets such as company reputation, culture, branding, and customer loyalty are crucial for continuous growth. The "two transformations" in 2000 laid a solid foundation for Company B to later transform itself into an integrated service supply chain operator.

3. **Third phase: Integrated services innovation (2001–2005)**

Company B became an integrated service supply chain player offering comprehensive business solutions to customers. It was involved in customer procurement, supply, technology, manufacturing, and other management functions, and helped customers integrate both internal and external resources. Specifically, the operations of Company B during this period had the following four major characteristics: (1) Company B shifted from selling machineries to offering total business solutions to its customers; (2) instead of internalizing different operations, Company B emphasized on integrating internal and external resources; (3) Company B moved from a transactions-driven customer relationship to one that focused on long-term services; and (4) Company B transformed itself from a manufacturer to a virtual manufacturing network operator. In 2005, of the RMB 2.5 billion total output value of Company B, 44% came from traditional manufacturing operations and the remaining was derived from services.

4. **Fourth phase: Expansion of service supply chain operations (2006–present)**

The service supply chain operations of Company B have evolved. Company B further extended its service supply chain operations with a major focus on strengthening the management of suppliers and distributors to enhance external resource management. It has also launched a real-time information sharing platform for different parties in the service supply chain. Another important change is the integration of capital flow with physical and information flows. Today, Company B considers supply chain financing management as a new direction for growth.

Industry Analysis

The industrial blower industry plays an important role in China's national economy. Industrial blowers are mainly used for the compression and transportation of gas; they have wide applications in oil, petrochemical, metallurgy, electricity, coal mining, construction, textiles, and transportation industries. The major products of the industrial blower industry include centrifugal compressors, centrifugal blowers, root blowers, centrifugal ventilating machines, axial ventilating machines, and other special-use ventilating machines. The industrial blower industry has been growing along with the opening up of the Chinese economy. In particular, the industry enjoyed huge growth opportunities in China's Eleventh Five-year plan period, during which economic restructuring was the focus of development—China would invest heavily in infrastructure, and industries such as petrochemical, metallurgy, and electricity would continue to play major roles in national economic development. It is believed that in the next five to ten years, major progress would be made in the technology, product, and industrial structure of China's industrial blower industry. In particular, the manufacturing of high-pressure, high-volume turbine compressors (including centrifugal compressors, axial compressors, and the centrifugal and axial compressors) has drawn major attention. Indeed, turbine compressors are important in many large-scale engineering projects, such as blast furnace smelting plants, coal plants, fertilizer plants, ethylene plants, air separation plants, natural gas pipelines, and oil field injection projects.

According to incomplete statistical data, between 1980 and 1996, the average annual increase in China's industrial blower production was 13.8%. In 2005, around 2.6–2.9 million industrial blowers were manufactured in China; of these, 1.6–1.8 million were centrifugal compressors and 0.26 million were axial compressors. The number of industrial blowers manufactured climbed to around 3.1–3.3 million in 2010; of these, 2.0–2.2 million were centrifugal compressors and 3.6 million were axial compressors.

In 2005, there were 383 industrial blower enterprises above the designated size in China. The enterprises achieved revenue sales of RMB 19 billion, an increase of 24.7% yoy; and their profits reached RMB 12.7 billion, an increase of 36.5% yoy. Major domestic turbine compressor manufacturers and operators include Shenyang Blower Works Group Corporation, Shaanxi Blower (Group) Company Limited, Shanghai Blower Works Company Limited, Chongqing General Industry (Group) Company Limited, Zhejian Shangfeng Industrial Holding Limited, and Wuhan Blower Company Limited; these companies own 50% of the total market share. Most of the other industrial blower companies are small- and medium- sized township-level enterprises with poor technological expertise.

Apart from domestic demand, China's industrial blowers are beginning to win acceptance in overseas markets. Since 2000, export sales have been growing by 5% per year. Between 1991 and 2000, the increase in the export of centrifugal compressors and blowers was relatively impressive; 87 centrifugal compressors and blowers were exported in 2000 and the major export destinations were emerging markets such as India, Pakistan, Iran, and Vietnam.

In terms of resources and capability, Company B focuses on providing demand-driven solutions, offering services such as installation, professional maintenance, and remote surveillance; Company B also provides services such as logistics distribution and order management, although these are not the core businesses of Company B. Indeed, the key customers of Company B are in the steel, petrochemical, and metallurgical industries. For these customers, effective system installations, and safe and stable production are the top priorities. Company B emphasizes the capabilities that its customers need the most.

The macro-environment in China is favorable for the development of the industrial blower industry. Large-scale engineering projects in the country are boosting the demand for high-end industrial blowers. Besides, the Chinese government is highly supportive toward the development of the industrial blower industry. Company B has a strong brand with a long company history starting in 1968; its products and services are widely recognized. Over the decades, Company B has developed close relationships with its customers.

As seen, although there is competition in the industrial blower industry in China, the overall prospect is positive; and the Chinese government supports the development of the industry as well. With strong demand of management capability helping customers realize smooth production, Company B is in a very good position. Indeed, customers tend to put stronger emphasis on cost reduction at a system-wide level through effective services and operations, instead of squeezing prices of single product items. It would be correct to say that the risks Company B faces, such as operations risks, are more at a micro-level.

Service Supply Chain Strategy of Company B

Driven by constant changes in the competitive environment, manufacturing enterprises are prompted to offer more flexible solutions based on their core competencies. Instead of the traditional pyramid management structure, more and more manufacturing enterprises are adopting the horizontal management structure, which grants more flexibility and discretion to individual units to boost creativity. Besides, the competitive relationships between enterprises are changing. In the past, many viewed competition as a zero-sum game. But today, more and more enterprises hope to build collaborative win-win relationships—information sharing and integration of internal and external resources are regarded as the key to success. This trend is tearing down many traditional barriers between different enterprises, as well as between enterprises and customers. In fact, the "two transformations" strategy launched by Company B was a direct response to the changing trend; Company B redesigned its supply chain operations model.

Sales and marketing lead the supply chain operations

In the past, Company B focused primarily on product manufacturing, development, and sales. Operation models had been fairly passive—Company B awaited orders from customers before initiating a series of operations such as manufacturing, installation, and distribution. Supply chain services received little attention. However, this started to change in 2001, when the company revamped its old model and began to actively explore the needs of its customers. The whole operating model became more customer-driven.

More specifically, apart from manufacturing machineries, Company B also offers service packages (including system design, provision of system facilities, system installation, and testing) as well as contracting in engineering (including basic facilities, factories, and external facilities construction). Company B essentially offers total solutions to its customers. For instance, in the top pressure recovery turbines manufacturing project for Baosteel Group Corporation, Company B was also responsible for the construction of auxiliary facilities, factories, basic and external facilities, as well as blast furnace waste heat recovery power generation. The benefits for the customer were clear. First, the customer was relieved from the heavy workload of coordinating with different parties such as manufacturers, auxiliary facilities providers, engineering operators, and so on, since Company B would be responsible for these tasks. Second, it could better control the project investment and investment cycles, and effectively solve the problem of cost increase due to incompatible systems and lack of experiences. The marketing department, the sales department, as well as the engineering contracting department of Company B would take the lead in understanding customer requirement, and propose the contract details for the approval of the contract management center (Exhibit 4.8).

Exhibit 4.8: Service Supply Chain Model of Company B

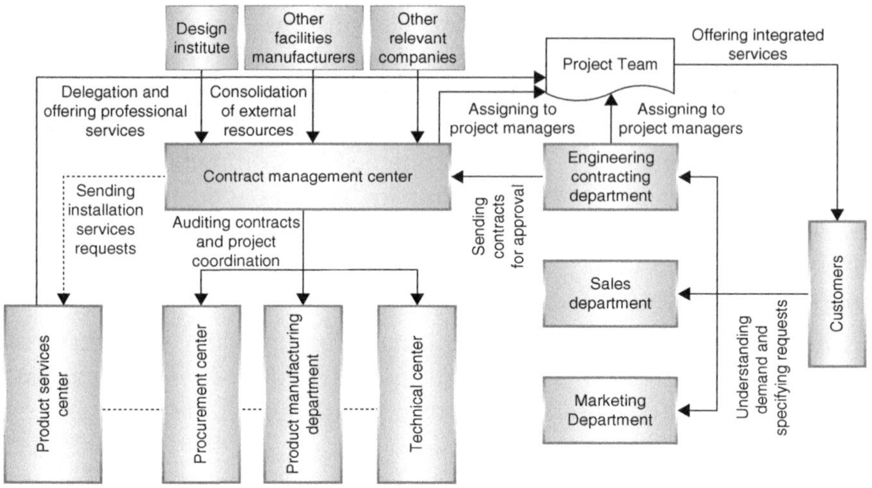

Coordination and consolidation of internal supply chain activities

After understanding customer needs and demand consolidation, Company B needs to review the proposed contract details carefully in order to control its operating risks. Effective coordination and consolidation of activities between different departments is critical to smoothen internal supply chain operations. The contract management center of Company B is responsible for coordinating with different supply chain activities; the center has three major roles. The first role includes planning, forecasting, and compiling contract details. These works are conducted on an annual, quarterly, and monthly basis.

Generally speaking, each year, the contract management center will work on the master contract plan (such as ordering and manufacturing plans) for the next year based on forecasts that take into account a number of parameters such as the socioeconomic situation and customer factors. After formulating the master contract details, the center will work on the more detailed quarterly planning, taking into considerations product performance, loans, relative importance of customers, auxiliary facilities, and so on. Then, based on the quarterly plans, monthly plans will be created; the contract management center will coordinate with relevant departments or units (such as procurement and supply, and production) to find the right balance between demand and supply.

The second role of the contract management center is contract implementation. Different factors such as order size and requirements can complicate contract implementation. Thus, it is crucial to explain to customers beforehand the contract details, especially the sales contracts. Next, the contract management center will delegate job duties to relevant departments or units; when needed, training may be provided to help relevant departments or units fully understand the requirements of customers and the potential problems that may arise during contract implementation.

The third role of the contract management center is offering guidance to, as well as managing and coordinating with the engineering contracting, sales, and marketing departments. Sufficient communication between different internal departments and units is regarded as the key to meeting customer requirements. The contract management center will preliminarily review every contract proposed, offer guiding sales suggestions and standards, and designate the delivery period. Sales and marketing departments are allowed to sign contracts with customers directly, but the contracts must be approved by the contract management center should the delivery period be longer than the designated benchmarks. Besides, the contract management center will offer constant feedback to sales and marketing departments, and rearrange internal activities to ensure effective operations.

Procurement

The first task after contract order approvals by the contract management center is procurement. Well-executed procurement offers strong support production and other successive operations; procurement has a major impact on company competitiveness. The procurement of Company B is relatively complex, and involves four main product categories: (1) raw materials, which include mainly steel and non-ferrous metals; (2) auxiliary materials such as petrochemicals; (3) auxiliary parts such as mortars and seals; and (4) other product supplies. Company B has different procurement systems for these products.

Steel accounts for a relatively small share of procurement; hence, Company B mainly opts for steel procurement in-house. On the other hand, Company B adopts a zero-inventory model for auxiliary materials; the company outsources its procurement of auxiliary materials to several third parties and is in charge of price auditing. Company B outsources the procurement of auxiliary materials mainly because there are huge variations in material prices and quality; in-house procurement would create heavy workloads without adding much value to the company. Outsourcing procurement of the auxiliary materials can greatly simplify procurement operations and enhance company competitiveness. To effectively manage procurement outsourcing, Company B carries out various processes to reinforce product and management quality, such as training, sampling checks, and system audits. The technical center of Company B will issue a technical agreement; and the company also sets standards on delivery period, quality, after-sales services, and so on. As for procurement logistics, Company B adopts the VMI approach—suppliers assume full responsibility for maintaining an agreed inventory of the materials in Xi'an, so that they can fulfill the order requests from Company B immediately; Company B pays the suppliers later.

Company B mainly employs bidding and price comparison approaches for the procurement of auxiliary parts, such as pipeline valves and transmissions. The company prepays a certain amount of guarantee fees to its suppliers, and will arrange full payments after delivery and quality assurance. Company B does not maintain inventory for regular auxiliary parts; suppliers will directly install the parts for the company onsite. The procurement center will carry out quality checks and audits according to different quality assurance benchmarks.

Project management

Company B provides integrated services to its customers; since this involves several procedures and operations, management is a complicated task. Effective project management is crucial for success. Therefore, after auditing and project formulations, the contract management center will also take the initiative to establish project teams to oversee different business units and activities. The project teams will visit different customer locations to monitor the project progress and to effectively allocate resources.

Company B also implements a two-tier management system. After signing the engineering service contracts with customers, the engineering contracting center will assign a project manager for each project to monitor onsite progress; the project manager is effectively made responsible to make operations decisions on a discretionary basis. The engineering contracting center would provide project management guidelines to managers. Besides, the contract management center will also delegate another project manager to oversee the project. Most project managers delegated by the contract management center are retired technicians and managers of Company B with extensive work experience and are well-versed in company operations. The project managers from the engineering contracting center and the contract management center share different management scopes: managers from the engineering contracting center focus on onsite project management, while managers from the engineering contracting center mainly focus on coordination of internal resources. The results of the two-tier management system are very impressive; Company B sees major improvements in its customer service standards.

Customer services

In the supply chain operations of Company B, the product service center plays a very important role. The center was originally responsible for the maintenance of the company's own engineering facilities, but since the launch of the two transformations strategy, the center has outsourced the maintenance functions to professional service providers and transformed itself into a specialty unit for full supply chain services. The original team is reassigned to provide maintenance services for customers, which create higher added value for the company. The major roles of the center in supply chain operations include the following: (1) the center working with other business units or departments during the contract implementation process to form project teams to assist the installation and testing of machineries; (2) arranging maintenance services for different machines and facilities; and (3) offering customized solutions for its customers, which covers not only the machineries by Company B, but also other customer facilities and products upon requests.

Service Supply Chain Management Components of Company B

The operations management model of Company B fully exemplifies the service supply chain management philosophy.

Integrated demand and customer relationship management

Integrated demand and customer relationship management focus on the following three areas: (1) system sales services launched by Company B since 2001, (2) maintenance services, and (3) remote surveillance. To optimize resources usage and reduce costs, Company B outsourced the maintenance of its own engineering facilities and at the same time, the original team was re-assigned to provide professional maintenance services to customers; in particular, the team offers system services that also include the maintenance of machines and facilities other than those manufactured by Company B. This brings huge costs savings to customers. The stability and safety operations of turbine machines are critical for customer system operations. In the past, Company B offered only maintenance services when problems arose; this undoubtedly caused disruptions in customer operations. Since the launch of the "two transformations" strategy, Company B took a more proactive precautionary approach—it developed a rotating surveillance system and a computer diagnostic system, which enable the company to conduct real-time remote monitoring of machine operations via the Internet. Its professional teams of technicians would also be on 24/7 standby and compile regular operations reports for customers. The systems can help the customers accurately grasp the overall operations and swiftly arrange replacement and maintenance schedules to ensure uninterrupted business operations; besides, they can also focus their attention on core business operations. On the other hand, the professional teams and systems help Company B attain leadership positions in sales and marketing efforts.

Inventory management

Inventories can serve as buffers to meet market uncertainties. However, the traditional inventory management model has a major disadvantage of underutilization and mismanagement of suppliers' resources, which ties up working capital and adds to operation risks. Therefore, Company B opts for establishing strategic partnerships with major raw material suppliers, and has launched a zero-inventory management model for its raw materials; suppliers would help manage inventory for Company B. Suppliers will deliver the raw materials to Company B according to its production schedules; Company B will later pay to the suppliers based on usage volume. According to statistics from the procurement center of Company B, the zero inventory management model had helped Company B reduce working capital tie-ups by as much as RMB 1.33 million in 2004.

Apart from strengthening the management of its raw materials supply, Company B also sought to optimize the spare parts inventory of its customers. The blower machine items of Company B usually form the core parts of customers' operations. To prevent major disruptions, customers would usually keep spare units for replacement, particularly for some fragile items. However, this causes tie-up of working capital and storage problems. To solve these problems, Company B offers zero inventory services for spare items for its customers. For instance, with the spare parts services by Company B, Laigang Group Company no longer needs to keep inventory for spare parts; in case of emergency replacement needs, Company B can provide the items immediately. The benefits to Laigang Group Company are obvious: There are no working capital tie-up or storage costs, and there are no concerns about operations disruptions. For Company B, as the parts can be used in its wide collection of products with little reprocessing, it can offer zero inventory services for many of its customers with timely response. The customers will share the benefits of efficiency gains from the services along with Company B. The spare parts services, indeed, became a new profit source for Company B. According to company statistics, between 2002 and 2004, the value of the order from the spare parts services totaled RMB 124 million; the average annual increase was 45%.

Supplier relationship management

The integrated supply chain solutions offered by Company B involve a great deal of supplier coordination and management. For instance, in an RMB 12 million project, Company B itself was only involved directly in a small part

(RMB 0.5 million) and outsourced the bulk of the project to third-party services providers. Effective supplier relationship management is crucial for integrated services. Company B has dedicated teams in different regions of China to locate suitable suppliers for different projects. Before signing any service contract for customers, Company B will visit and assess potential suppliers in advance; different departments such as operations and finance are involved to ensure comprehensive assessment to lower execution risks. Company B not only evaluates factors such as technical capability, integrity, and company culture, but is also involved in project budgeting. Company B believes that it is important to not only solely consider price factors during the tender process as it is likely to bring negative impacts on quality. To fully satisfy customers' requirement, it is crucial to assess, analyze, and manage every operation process and control the costs to ensure quality services.

Company B has a standing unit responsible for building strategic collaborations with suppliers. The standing unit convenes annual meetings to introduce to suppliers the company culture and strategy of Company B; the latest R&D trends in system technology are also discussed. Besides, there are monthly meetings between representatives from different departments such as quality control, procurement, technology, finance, and so on, and some members from the standing unit, to share with one another the latest developments in operations and issues such as financing and delivery mode. The standing unit also invites suppliers to rate the performance of different departments and evaluate the operations process of Company B so that the company can constantly improve its operations process to boost efficiency.

Capacity management

Service supply chain operations rely heavily on integrated management of different capacities. In September 2003, Company B established a "system technology and facilities collaborative network" in Xian with 56 ancillary companies to facilitate resources and knowledge sharing; some well-known companies include Siemens and General Electric. Through collaborative relationships, Company B also enhances the quality of its human resources. For instance, one of the ancillary companies offers to provide human resource training to 50 employees of Company B every year in its Singapore base; Formosa Plastics Corporation also provides annual human resources trainings to 20 employees of Company B in Taiwan.

Besides, to strengthen its R&D capability, Company B collaborates with universities and research institutes through joint development efforts and commission auditing. It also works closely with its ancillary companies on system technology developments. For instance, its "blast furnace top gas pressure stability analysis of the top pressure in power generation equipment and control experimental study" with Zhejiang University has a registered patent in China; its large-scale air separation devices supporting compressors co-developed with MAN Diesel & Turbo from Germany are also very well-received in the market.

Capital and financing management

Capital and financing management has been in the spotlight in recent years and is one of the integral elements in service supply chain operations. Apart from integrated supply chain services, Company B also provides supply chain financing management services. Since 2004, Company B has established strategic partnerships with many banks including the Industrial and Commercial Bank of China, Shanghai Pudong Development Bank, and China Merchants Bank, to provide financing and credit risk services for its customers.

Company B has established an accounting center to centrally manage different accounts and consolidate funds and repay loans. Company B works with banks to strengthen capital management. Indeed, due to huge cash flows of Company B, any percentage change in interest rate can mean gains or losses in revenue by around tens of millions of dollars; thus, strong portfolio management of the capital are necessary to maximize the financial performance of the company.

Company B has also established a contract management center and a financial center to launch supply chain financing services in collaboration with banks, which seek to centrally integrate the physical, information, and funding flows in supply chain operations to improve operating efficiency and reduce operating capital and risks. Using its own capital as well as bank credits, Company B offers fixed asset-based (e.g., facilities) and warehouse receipts-based (e.g., steel) financing services to its core customers. For instance, Rizhao Steel Group did not have sufficient capital for a project involving the building of six blast furnaces; it could only pay 15% of the contract payment and opted for repaying the rest of the money from future revenue derived from the project. Most companies would have found this type of financing arrangement too risky. However, based on a thorough understanding of its core customers, Company B was willing to provide supply chain financing to the Rizhao Steel Group. Company B sent representatives from its different departments to visit the customer onsite and make relevant mortgage and legal assessments. Eventually, the project went ahead with the approval of the Xi'an local government. Generally speaking, Company B would first cooperate with commercial banks to evaluate the financial risks and put forward a suitable financing plan to ensure repayment by phases. In its project with the Rizhao Steel Group, Company B collected the first batch of loan money as production kicked off; as the operations become more mature, Company B borrowed from banks using the facilities and warehouse receipts of Rizhao Steel Group as collaterals, and offered financing for the steel company. Company B and its sub-contractors share the risks and benefits of the supply chain financing services.

The Results

Before 2000, Company B was a traditional blower manufacturing and operating enterprise with poor market competitiveness and was vulnerable to market changes. However, since the two transformations strategy implemented in 2000, the company witnessed significant progress in operating efficiency and competitiveness. In 2009, the total assets of Company B reached RMB 3.45 billion, registering an increase of RMB 2.53 billion compared to that in 2000; the net assets of Company B were RMB 932 million, a 4.14-fold increase compared to that in 2000. In 2000, Company B had 3,326 employees and it achieved a total output value of RMB 340 million and profit of RMB 14 million. In 2009, Company B had 2,969 employees (an 11% decrease compared to that in 2000), but it realized total sales revenue of RMB 3.6 billion and profit of RMB 460 million.

All in all, Company B serves its customers by consolidating the resources and services of the supply chains. As we will see, customers of Company B pay major attention to ensure smooth supply chain operations; rather than on the prices of single machinery items, they place strong emphasis on the cost control of overall operations. Strong capacity management is crucial. In this regard, Company B leverages its expertise and collaborates with upstream design institutes, other facilities manufacturers, and suppliers to build a service supply chain network and provide integrate services to downstream customers. The service supply chain model of Company B is one that features business processes integration to offer total solutions to customers (Exhibit 4.9).

Exhibit 4.9: Service Supply Chain Model Featuring Business Processes Integration to Offer Total Solutions

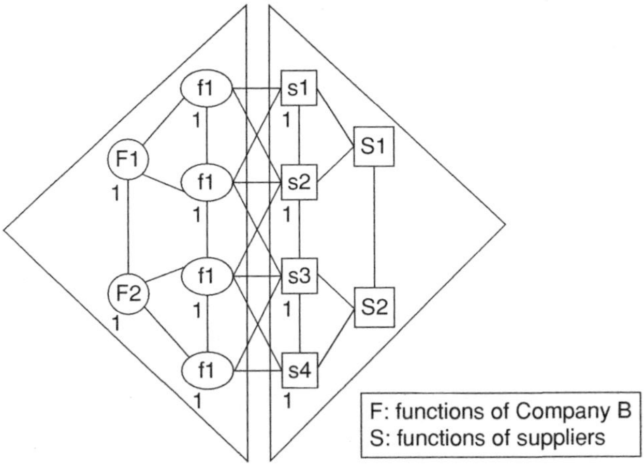

Case Study: Service Supply Chain Model Featuring Integrated Modular Services—The Service Supply Chain of Company S

Integrated modular service model features a platform that integrates different modules such as logistics services, goods services, information services, fund services, organizational management, financial management, quality management, and performance management; the aim is to satisfy diverse customer requirements through customized modules.

Company Background

The steel production services industry encompasses operations of all the processes of the steel industry, including resources development, transportation and logistics, raw materials supply, sintering, iron and steel refining, continuous casting, and product sales. Company S was founded by the merging of several state companies in February 1993 with the approval from the former Economic and Trade Office of the State Council. The State Bureau of Metallurgical Industry also later merged dozens of metallurgical companies into Company S. However, in the first ten years of operations, Company S had not taken its unique historical advantages to offer integrated services for metallurgical companies. It was only after 2004 that Company S responded to market changes and positioned itself as an integrated services provider for steel companies. Besides, the company also strengthened its relationship with five industries closely connected with the steel industry, including mining, carbon, refractory, ferroalloy, and machinery and equipment manufacturing industries to establish services including the development and processing of metallurgical mineral resources, metallurgical raw materials, trade and logistics, related engineering services, and equipment manufacturing. From 2004 onward, Company S took steps to enhance specialization and internationalization.

Industry Analysis

According to the structure-conduct-performance approach in industrial organization theory, the structure of an industry determines the conduct of its firms, and the conduct of the firms determines an industry's performance (Bain 1956). Elements of an industry structure include the growth rate of market demand, barriers to entry, product differentiation, and seller concentration. Company S is mainly geared toward catering to the steel industry, which can be sub-divided into categories such as mining, sintering, raw materials and equipment, continuous casting, and sales and logistics. The level of product differentiation is high. Besides, due to the high degree of specialization, heavy requirements of technological knowledge, and its capital-intensive nature, there are high barriers to entry in the steel industry.

Boosted by the growing demand from China and other emerging economies as well as credit expansion, China's steel industry has shown rapid expansion in recent years. China's crude steel production has jumped by more than fourfold from 128 million tons in 2000 to 570 million tons in 2009. Despite huge steel production capacity in China, industry developments in China lag behind its foreign counterparts. Many of the country's steel manufacturers produce low-end steel products. In fact, many manufacturers still use outdated production methods and facilities that have already been phased out internationally. Energy consumption in steel production in China is 15%–20% higher than that in advanced economies, and effective utilization of resources is 20%–40% lower.

China has many steel manufacturers; however, most of them are small- and medium-sized. In 2010, there were 32 steel manufacturers with crude steel production capacity of over 3 million tons, 24 manufacturers with production capacity of over 5 million tons, 9 manufacturers with production capacity of over 10 million tons in China. Only 4 manufacturers had production capacity of over 20 million tons, and these included Hebei Iron and Steel Group, Baosteel Group, Anshan Iron and Steel Group, and Wuhan Iron and Steel Group. Only Hebei Iron and Steel Group and Baosteel Group achieved crude steel production of over 30 million tons; crude steel production in 2009 was 33.4 million and 31.5 million tons, respectively. Seller concentration is low. In the beginning of 2010, these four steel manufacturers occupied less than 20% of the total market share in China. In developed economies such as the United States, the European Union, and Japan, the domestic market share of the top four steel manufacturers is usually above 60%–70%.

Steel manufacturers are highly resource-dependent. In contrast to the low market concentration of steel manufacturers, market concentration of the upstream players is very high. Thus, steel manufacturers are in a disadvantageous position in business negotiations with high transaction costs. Let us consider iron ore as an example. In 2009, China imported 627 million tons of iron ore, an increase of 41.6% yoy; foreign trade dependence was as high as 69%. In the first seven months of 2011, China's iron ore import increased slightly by 1.5% yoy to 360 million tons. Driven by strong demand, the iron ore price once reached a historical high of USD 190 per ton; the iron ore prices stayed at a high level of USD 150 per ton for a long time. In fact, over 75% of the global iron ore production and trade were controlled by the "Big 3" iron ore producers—Rio Tinto, BHP Billiton, and Vale S.A.; the companies have a very strong say in price negotiations.

As seen, Company S is in an industry with a fairly extensive supply chain. The industry scale is large, but there is a huge imbalance between the supply and demand side, which poses high risks for industry players.

In terms of resources and capability, Company S provides resource exploration, trade and logistics, engineering technology, and equipment manufacturing services for steel manufacturing enterprises. Due to the scarcity of resources and market fluctuations, its customers set high standards on supply, effectiveness of business operations, and integration and inventory management. In terms of macro-institutional environment, as mentioned earlier, government policies have huge influences on the developments of the steel industry. Huge market imbalance and fluctuations in global economy (in particular, the recent spike in iron ore prices) have often necessitated government interventions. Facing relatively high risks, the transaction costs of the industry is high. For the customers of Company S, the key concern is how to lower transaction costs and ensure the stable supply of materials and products.

Service Supply Chain Network Structure and Strategy of Company S

Company S explored a new model for service supply chain operations. First, it sought to strengthen its internal capabilities through acquiring and merging with manufacturing enterprises in China that demonstrate a strong edge in resources and operations, which are in line with its core businesses. At the same time, it also established a stable procurement relationship with external suppliers for non-core business processes and products. Today, Company S has established five main business modules in mining, carbon, refractories, ferroalloy, and equipment manufacturing and has attained market leadership positions in these areas. Not only has Company S accumulated the "resources advantage," it has also strengthened its capability to offer integrated services for steel manufacturing companies. Company S has expanded its industry influence.

Through restructuring and mergers and acquisitions, Company S has "internalized" major R&D and manufacturing capabilities. Indeed, the company has developed a "multi-tier, multi-domain" customer demand response system targeting the steel manufacturing industry. There is a clear division of labor between different professional companies of Company S and the internal business processes based on business strategy; each business module operates within different professional streams, serving processes such as resource exploration, raw materials supply, trading, logistics and distribution, equipment manufacturing, product sales, and so on. Through its central information system platform, Company S monitors and controls its internal business processes and facilitates communication between its different units.

Specifically, the service supply chain network structure of Company S is a spider model (Exhibit 4.10). The 14 professional companies form the "trunk," while the local companies form the "nodes"; the corporate development unit of the headquarter serves as the central point. The information platform backed by the enterprise resource planning (ERP) system facilitates communications and collaborations between different companies and the corporate development unit to maximize value creations.

Exhibit 4.10: The Supply Chain Network Structure of Company S

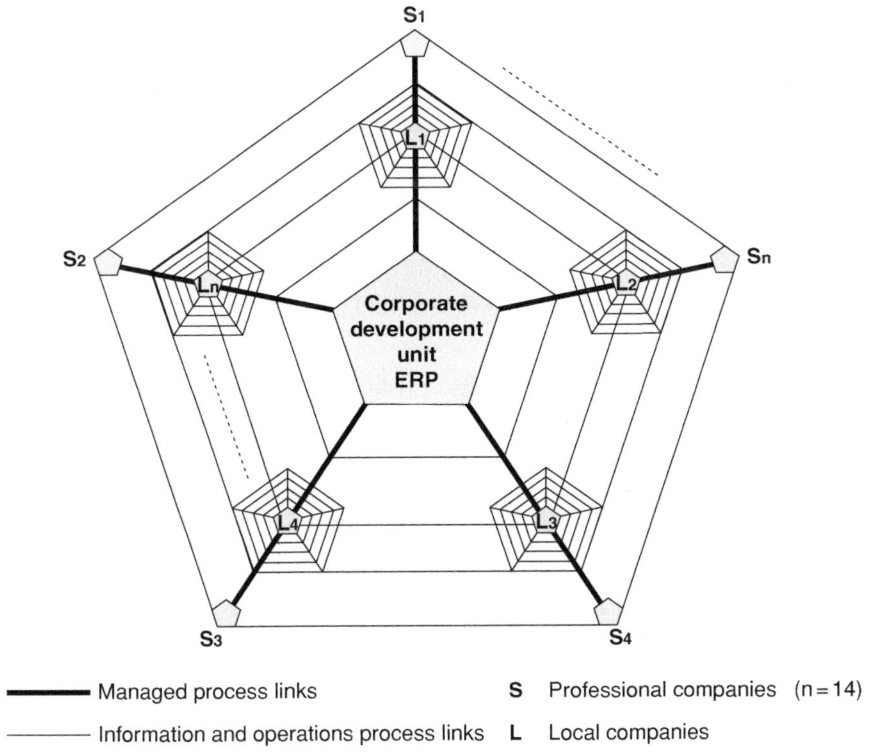

Corporate development unit: The center point of the service supply chain network

Company S is affiliated with different companies: professional companies, local companies, production enterprises, overseas enterprises, and technology enterprises. The company headquarters controls the decision-making on strategic planning, investment, financing, and human resources. Meanwhile, its affiliated companies have substantial discretionary power on daily production and operations activities—they can make all production and operations decisions unless those specified in advance by the headquarters.

The corporate development unit of the headquarters is the center point of the service supply chain network that is responsible for corporate strategic planning, management of affiliated companies, newly established companies, suppliers and customers, coordinating business activities, as well as performance assessments of different companies. Business operations and market information is sent to the corporate development unit via the ERP system for the unit to monitor the process links between affiliated companies.

For instance, the corporate development unit monitors and makes decisions on the collaborative activities between professional and local companies. If there are overlapping roles and operations, the corporate development unit will coordinate with the two parties. There are three major ways to resolve the issue, which are based on the following:

1. **Division of labor in the supply chain**
Although they handle the same products, local and professional companies focus on different phases of the supply chain operations. Professional companies are responsible for major operations process of core products, while local companies are mainly responsible for trading and customer-facing activities.

2. **Customer classifications**
Strategic customers are served by professional companies; meanwhile, professional companies entrust and collaborate with local companies to serve general customers. On the other hand, for new accounts developed by local companies, local companies can directly engage in some types of sales activities with these new customers.

3. **Performance assessment system**
The corporate development unit sets the performance targets for different local companies and may close down local companies that fail to meet the targets. There are also incentives to encourage collaborations between local and professional companies. Undoubtedly, the corporate development unit also spends tremendous efforts to promote conservation of human and financial resources in collaborations.

Professional and local companies: The "trunk" and "node" of the service supply chain network

Professional Companies

Currently, professional companies mainly position themselves for the import/export as well as the domestic trade of core products, manufacturing of internal orders, procurement for local companies, and formulating sales plans. They are also responsible for the overseas procurement of core materials.

Company S has detailed and professional internal division of labor with no overlapping operations between different professional companies. There is professional division of labor between different operations processes as well, with collaborative operations mechanisms governing supply chain operations among professional companies, local companies, production enterprises, technological enterprises, and overseas enterprises.

The 14 professional companies forming the "trunk" of the spider model are: Company S Trading, Company S Materials, Company S Iron and Steel, Company S Equipment, Company S Investment, Company S International Freight Forwarding, Company S Mining, Company S Tendering, Company S Consulting, Company S Technology Development, Company S Futures Brokerage, Company S Property Management, Company S Asset Management, and Company S Iron and Steel Trading. These professional companies have attained leadership positions in their respective fields and they have important positions in the operations structure of Company S. Indeed, they form the backbone of the entire service supply chain of the company. Production enterprises sell their products, and technological enterprises sell some of their products through professional companies. Professional companies conduct sales and procurement activities in different regions in China through local companies, and they conduct import and exports sales with the help of overseas companies.

Different professional companies grow together through collaborative operations. We see major improvement in the efficiency of different operations modules. Company S International Freight Forwarding, for instance, used to demonstrate average performance in China; however, when Company S consolidated and delegated all internal logistics operations to the freight forwarding company, its operating performance registered significant improvements. The freight forwarding company centrally manages the warehouses as well as inventories of different local companies. On one hand, centralized management helps strengthen monitoring and reduces warehouse pilferage. On the other hand, consolidated demand boosts the scale and influence of the freight forwarding company—the market share of the company in water transportation has climbed to rank three from its original rank in the twenties. Take another example: Since taking charge of all internal tendering operations, Company S Tendering ranked second in the industry.

Besides, the internal sales channel has sharpened the competitive edge of Company S. The problem of raw material shortages can completely halt the production of many manufacturing enterprises. However, Company S is in a better position than its competitors with the internal sales channels. Facilitated by collaborations between business modules, swift internal reallocation of raw materials helps production enterprises enhance management and lower transaction costs. Company S, too, has reinforced its service provisions capability.

Local Companies

Local companies are responsible for the sales and procurement of the non-core products of Company S, execution of procurement and sales plans of the core products for professional companies, execution of internal orders, customer and supplier services, local market research, and internal capability management. Local companies are not under any of the professional companies; however, they play a crucial role connecting local customers with different professional companies based on customer demand. Indeed, local companies have a finger on the pulse of the latest market developments, while the strength of professional companies lies in resources. Under the monitoring of the corporate development unit, they work effectively to serve the customers and maximize value creations.

The role of local companies varies. For instance, the local company in a region with rich iron and steel resources works more closely with Company S Trading; on the other hand, the local company in a region with rich ferroalloy resources works with Company S Materials on a frequent basis. One can say that local companies are the most flexible in operations within Company S. Except for the local companies in Shanghai, Tianjin, and Shenzhen, the establishment of all the other local companies is dependent on the operating performance—the corporate development unit sets benchmarks on operating performance based on market situations (the basic standards are sales revenue and profit of over RMB 500 million and RMB 5 million, respectively, in the first year of operations). Local companies will be closed down if they fail to meet the targets in the first two years of operations. To enhance flexibility, workers in local companies work on a contract basis and need to have their contracts renewed every year. Besides, the commercial properties of local companies are all purchased in the name of Company S instead of local companies.

The ERP system

Enabling real-time information sharing, the ERP system integrates internal management information across the entire company, embracing major operation modules such as financial accounting, management accounting, manufacturing planning and management, materials management, and sales and distribution, with an aim to facilitate the flow of information between all business functions within the boundaries of the organization to optimize resource allocation and improve operating efficiency. The information platform backed by the ERP system is a major enabler for Company S to monitor and coordinate different business functions. Exhibit 4.11 demonstrates the central monitoring system of Company S.

Exhibit 4.11: The Central Monitoring System of Company S

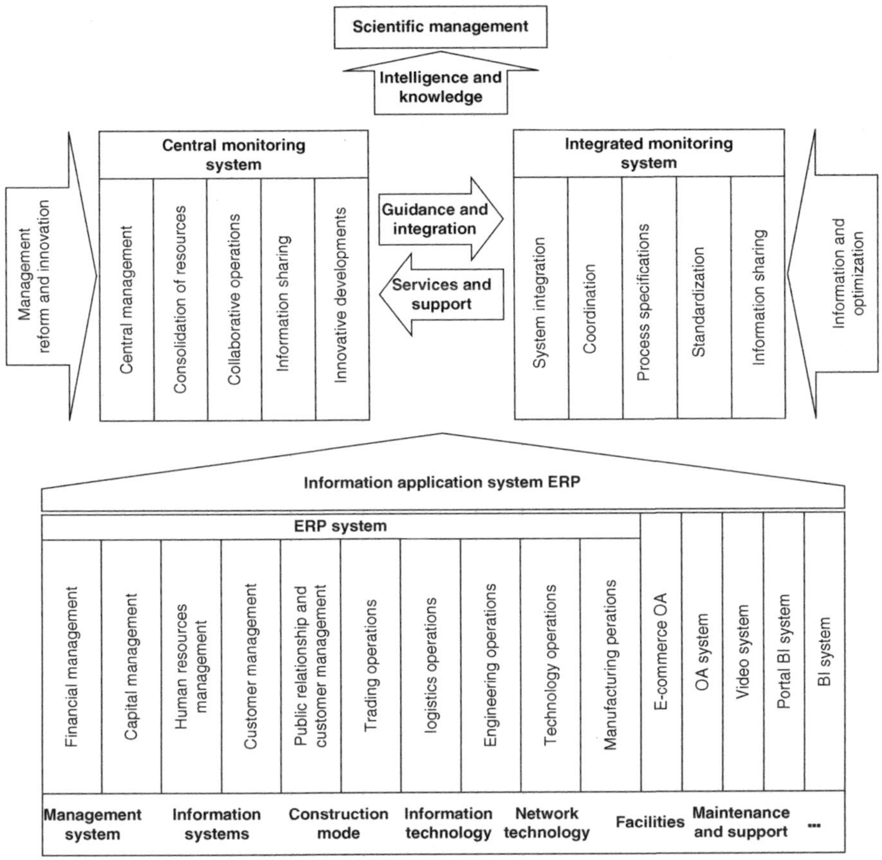

The adoption of the ERP system brings three major benefits: (1) it centralizes the management platform of Company S and standardizes the operation processes and the management model; (2) through a standardized information system, it facilitates the coordination of different operation units as well as resources allocation with upstream and downstream players, and realizes the integration of capital flow, information flow, and physical flow; and (3) it supports Company S to manage different local companies.

All in all, the corporate development unit of the headquarters serves as the central point in Company S, while the professional companies and local companies form the "trunk" and the "nodes." Together, they form a spider model service supply chain network. The common information platform backed by the ERP system helps integrate internal and external resources. Company S has very strong integrated services capability, which is difficult for its competitors to imitate; it strives to maintain its competitive edge in different professional areas such as mining, carbon, refractory, engineering equipment, and ferroalloy.

The Results

Company S is in an industry where the external risks are very high. The key for companies to gain competitive edge in the market is to consolidate resources to provide integrated services at lower costs. This drove Company S to transform itself from a pure trading company to an integrated service provider. Following the transition, the annual operating income and total profit in 2007 jumped by 8.4 and 10.1 folds, respectively, from those in 2003. The rank of Company S in "China's Top 500 Companies" climbed from 150 in 2003 to 33 in 2008.

The service supply chain operations model of Company S is totally different from the previous three models we introduced. Given the uncertainties in the industrial and institutional environment, the service providers' ability to effectively supply limited resources is valued by customers. Customers are keen to lower the high transaction costs due to market uncertainties. Therefore, Company S seeks to strengthen its service capabilities through "internalization" of production and technology enterprises, which play core roles in the industry value chain through buying stakes and horizontal integration. At the same time, Company S also consolidates external resources by collaborating with suppliers, science and research institutes, and financial institutes.

Company S adopts a modularized service supply chain model (Exhibit 4.12). There are a number of service modules that comprise different service components and resources; Company S offers a combination of different service models to realize integrated services according to customer requirements.

Compatibility of Service Supply Chain Models and Service Characteristics

It is highly important for companies to adopt the right service supply chain models. Fisher (1997) divided products into two categories based on their demand patterns: functional and innovative; and suggested that companies must match the product types with the right supply chains, as incompatibility between product types and supply chain models will lower supply chain efficiency. Fisher's influential study provides invaluable insights into relationships between product types and supply chain models. However, there are two areas that deserve further attention: (1) the reasons behind the need to adopt different supply chain models for different products, and (2) Fisher's model focuses mainly on manufacturing supply chains, which cannot be directly extrapolated to service supply chains.

Exhibit 4.12: Service Supply Chain Models Featuring Modularized Services

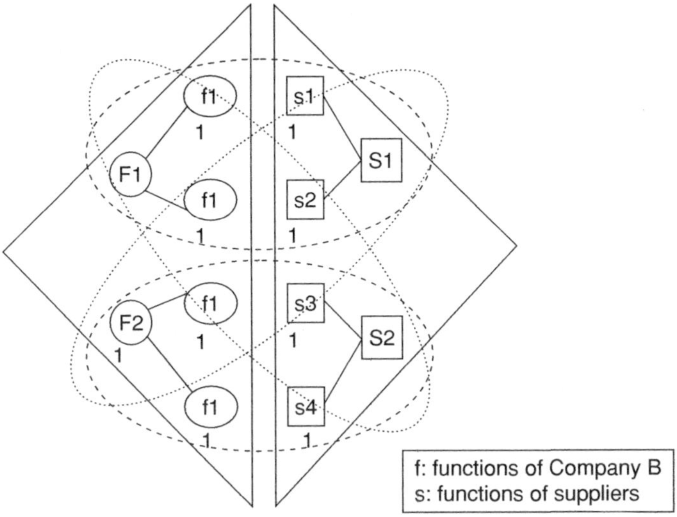

From our previous case studies, we can see that service supply chain operations models and the value propositions of customers vary by company and industry. There are many factors leading to uncertainties in service supply chains. From the perspective of organizations theory, there are two types of risks factors: internal and external. Internal factors are chiefly related to the resources and capabilities of companies, while the external factors are mainly related to the industry characteristics and institutional environment. Having extensive resources and capabilities tends to increase the complexity of the internal operations of companies. On the other hand, the greater the number of processes involved in the operations of an industry, the higher the odds of impeded information flow, which leads to higher transaction costs. Besides, the more frequent the changes in the external environment, the higher the policy risks companies have to bear. Customer requirements for service providers also vary by industry. Usually, customers are more price-sensitive in a competitive market environment. On the contrary, in less competitive but more complicated institutional environment, customers are less price-sensitive, and they tend to pay better attention to controlling overall transaction costs and enhancing competitiveness.

A compatible service supply chain model is crucial for companies to lower their supply chain risks and improve the operating performance. Resources, capabilities, industry characteristics, and institutional environment all imply different levels of supply risks. Besides, different degrees of price sensitiveness and value propositions of customers also affect customers' supply chain models. If companies face more internal supply chain operations risks, that is, they face high costs in the design, operations, management, and monitoring costs of supply chains then, to overcome the problem, companies may provide embedded services in their products or integrate business processes. This solution will help utilize different external resources on the basis of supply chain operations and the control of core resources and capabilities to improve the coordination of upstream and downstream players, better demand management, and optimize the supply chain costs. If companies face more external risks, that is, their transaction costs are high due to challenges such as bounded rationality, opportunism, and transaction frequency; then, to lower the risks, they may internalize the core resources and capabilities through seamlessly connected or modularized services to enhance flexibility. On the other hand, if customers are more price-sensitive, companies may consider offering embedded or seamlessly connected service as the bundling of different service elements creates better value for money; if they are more concerned with enhancing competitiveness, business process integration or modularized service models are a better option. As seen, a suitable service supply chain model is closely related to the value proposition of customers as well as the supply chain risks they faced (Exhibit 4.13). A mismatch of the service supply chain model drags down service efficiency and causes higher supply chain risks.

Exhibit 4.13: Service Supply Chain Models

		Supply chain risks	
		Operations risks	**Institutional risks**
Value propositions for customers	Price-sensitive	Service supply chain model featuring embedded services in products	Service supply chain model featuring seamless connections of different supply chain players
	Enhancing competitiveness	Service supply chain model featuring business processes integration	Service supply chain models featuring modularized services

Chapter 5
Service Outsourcing and Procurement in Service Supply Chains: Perspective of Service Buyers

Along with increasing servitization of businesses, more and more companies today are shifting from selling only products to offering integrated and customized products and services that deliver value in use. This change reflects, on one hand, the changing strategies of suppliers and their efforts to stay competitive in the market; on the other hand, it also reflects a change in the attitude of their customers to incorporate service procurement in their businesses, apart from the traditional goods-approach procurement. This change requires customers to have a systematic framework to handle their relationships with suppliers, and to have a clear picture of the services they need. In this chapter, we will explore, from the perspectives of service buyers, the determining factors behind service procurement and the level of outsourcing. We will also walk through the different forms of service procurement and outsourcing.

Service Procurement and Outsourcing

A typical value chain involves a combination of basic and auxiliary activities. It is often extremely difficult for companies to fulfill all basic and auxiliary activities at various stages of a value chain using only their own resources and capacity. Therefore, many companies often opt for outsourcing part of the businesses to other service providers, or to phrase it differently, procure services from third-party providers. In recent years, we have observed a growing trend of outsourcing services such as information technology, human resources, and logistics. Renowned outsourced service providers such as Hewitt Associates and Manpower Inc in the field of information technology; Flextronics and Foxconn in the field of contract manufacturing; and Sinotrans Shipping, COSCO, and UPS in the field of logistics services have brought great value to their customers. Indeed, the rise of service providers enables customers to focus on their core competencies through outsourcing non-core activities. And, as their businesses grow, service providers also benefit from better economy of scale and progress.

The definition of service outsourcing and procurement has evolved over the years. According to the business consulting firm, BearingPoint, outsourcing is an emerging service model in which companies delegate non-core businesses to external professional service providers with the support of information technology, and they utilize the knowledge and workforce of the service providers to complete tasks that were formerly conducted in-house. Outsourcing helps enterprises achieve cost reduction, increase efficiency, and improve market responsiveness by making the best out of limited resources. Li and Choi (2009) viewed service outsourcing as a choice of replacing internal service functions with the use of external agents to perform one or multiple service activities; service outsourcing is different from manufacturing outsourcing. The differences between goods and service procurement are also echoed by Van Der Valk and Rozemeijer (2009). Lovelock (1983) and Zeithaml and Bitner (1996) further pointed out that there are four unique characteristics of services, namely, intangibility, heterogeneity, inseparability, and perishability, which make service outsourcing distinctly different from manufacturing outsourcing. The intangible nature of services makes monitoring and measuring performance before and after purchase a difficult task for service buyers. Therefore, service providers need to help their customers develop a reference framework in order to review service performance. The inseparability of services chiefly means that production and consumption are simultaneous in services. Customers need to be present during service provisions and interact with the service providers. Indeed, customers are both consumers and cocreators of services. In this sense, it is often difficult to distinguish the rights and responsibilities of both parties. Ellram, Tate, and Billington (2004) believed that service processes depend to a large extent on the exchange of knowledge, expertise, and capabilities of human beings (which often varies); consequently, it is difficult to produce services with consistent characteristics and quality. Lastly, the fact that services cannot be inventoried adds to the difficulties of accurate planning and forecasting.

Li and Choi (2009) suggested that there are fundamental differences in the structural arrangements of service outsourcing and manufacturing. In manufacturing outsourcing, the customer is not in direct contact with suppliers. The manufacturing buyer acts as a bridge between customer and suppliers and has effective control on interactions between its supplier and customer. This relationship in a manufacturing supply chain can be represented as a linear diagram. Meanwhile, in service outsourcing, the service buyer, its customer, and supplier must interact with one another. This more complex relationship in a service supply chain can be represented as a triangular diagram (Exhibit 5.1).

Exhibit 5.1: Comparison of Supply Chain Triadic Relationship Structures in Manufacturing vs. Services

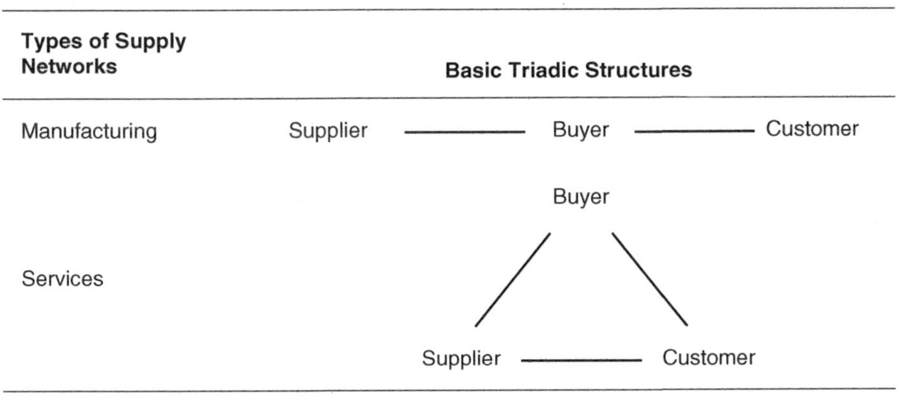

Because of the specific characteristics of service outsourcing, Blumenberg, Wagner, and Beimborn (2009) held the view that knowledge management is particularly important in service outsourcing. Indeed, knowledge transfers, effective mechanisms for integration between service providers and its suppliers, and the creation of shared knowledge are critical in service outsourcing (Bustinza, Molina, and Gutierrez-Gutierrez, 2010).

Classification of Service Outsourcing

Service outsourcing can be classified in different ways on the basis of the following.

Service content

Based on service content, service outsourcing includes Information Technology Outsourcing (ITO), Business Process Outsourcing (BPO), and Knowledge Process Outsourcing (KPO).

ITO can be a combination of product support and professional services to deliver information technology infrastructure, application services, or both to customers. BPO means the delegation of one, or more, information technology-intensive business processes to an external service provider that in turn owns, administers, and manages the selected process based on defined and measurable performance criteria. Examples include logistics, procurement, human resources, finance, accounting, customer relationship management, and other administrative or customer-facing business functions. KPO focuses on knowledge-intensive business processes that require significant domain expertise, analytical skills, and judgement to assist customers' decision-making.

Service location

Based on the outsourced service locations, service outsourcing can be classified into three types: onshore outsourcing, near-shore outsourcing, and offshore outsourcing.

Onshore outsourcing involves obtaining services from an external service provider within the same country (e.g., a US company outsources its work to an external service provider and the service is performed in the United States). If the work is performed by a service provider located geographically close to a company, it is called near-shore in-sourcing (e.g., a US company outsources its work to an external service provider and the service is performed in nearby countries in North America). Offshore outsourcing happens when a company has its outsourced work performed by an external party in a location far away from its country (e.g., a US company has its outsourced work performed in India, Russia, and China).

Peng (2009) also factored in geographical dimensions. Based on service location and modes (in-house or outsource), service activities can be classified into four types: off-shoring (international/foreign outsourcing), in-shoring (domestic outsourcing), captive sourcing (setting up subsidiaries abroad—the work is done in-house in a foreign location), and domestic in-house activity (Exhibit 5.2).

Types of outsourcing agreements

Millar (1994) put forward four types of outsourcing agreements: (1) general outsourcing (which includes three alternatives: selective outsourcing, value-added outsourcing, and cooperative outsourcing), (2) transitional outsourcing (which involves the migration from one technological platform to another), (3) business process outsourcing (in which a third party service provider is responsible for an entire business function for the customer's organization), and (4) business benefit contracting (which involves a contractual agreement that defines the service provider's contribution to the

Exhibit 5.2: Classification of Service Activities Based on Location and Mode

Mode of activity

Location of activity	*In-house*	*Outsourcing*	
	Cell 1 Captive sourcing / FDI	*Cell 2* Offshoring	*Foreign location*
	Cell 3 Domestic in-house	*Cell 4* Inshoring	*Domestic location*

customer in terms of specific benefits to the business and that the customer will make the payment based on the service provider's ability to deliver the benefits.

Willcocks and Lacity (1998), on the other hand, introduced six forms of "emerging sourcing arrangements": (1) value-added outsourcing (combining the strengths of the parties of the outsourcing arrangement to launch new products and services), (2) equity holding (one party acquires equity in the other), (3) multi-sourcing (one outsourcing contract for several service providers), (4) cosourcing (the revenue of the outsourcing service provider is linked to the performance of the company that it serves), (5) spin-offs (the internal information system department is converted into a new company and sells its services to the market, and (6) creative contracting (includes customized clauses to satisfy specific customer requirements).

As seen, there are various classifications for different outsourcing models. That said, the classifications do not explain in detail the driving forces behind different outsourcing decisions. There are several activities and management components in a service supply chain; customers are usually willing to outsource part of the services and conduct some of the activities in-house. We shall explore the driving forces behind service outsourcing and the extent of service outsourcing.

Resources and Capability Acquisitions in Service Outsourcing

Regardless of different service outsourcing decisions, the fundamental motivation behind a company to outsource to a service provider is to acquire the resources, capabilities, or knowledge of the latter through building long-term and stable collaborative relationships. As such, Bustinza, Molina, and Gutierrez-Gutierrez (2010) believed that we can explore the reasons behind service outsourcing from resource-based, capability-based, and knowledge-based aspects of a company.

Penrose's (1959) widely-acknowledged *The Theory of the Growth of the Firm* contributed significantly to the resource-based view of a company. For the first time, intangible assets have been incorporated into the understanding of a company. A company is understood as an administrative framework that links and coordinates the activities of numerous parties as a bundle of productive resources. Later, Barney (1991) defined company resources to include assets, capabilities, organizational processes, company attributes, information, and knowledge controlled by a company in order to gain sustained competitive advantage, to improve long-term efficiency and effectiveness. The resource-based view of a company drives the developments of the resource-advantage theory (Hunt and Morgan, 1995; 2004), a competition theory which sees resources as heterogeneous across firms and is imperfectly mobile. A company's objective is to obtain superior performance through resource consolidation. The resource-advance theory suggests that the company's resources are the major determining factor of its competitive advantage and profitability. Valuable, rare, difficult-to-imitate, non-tradable, and non-substitutable resources are the necessary conditions for companies to gain a competitive advantage; meanwhile, companies must be able to avoid or neutralize threats to sustain their competitive advantage.

Teece (2007) suggested that apart from difficult-to-imitate resources, companies must possess the ability to integrate, build, and reconfigure internal and external competences to address rapidly changing environments—the ability he refers to as dynamic capabilities. Indeed, constantly changing markets such as new customer demand and technology advances require the company to reconfigure its asset structure and accomplish the necessary internal and external transformation in order to stay ahead of the competition.

Day (1994) defined capabilities as a set of a "complex bundle of skills and accumulated knowledge, exercised through organizational processes that enable companies to coordinate activities and make use of their assets."

Depending on the orientation and focus of the defining process, there are three types of capabilities: inside-out (internal), outside-in (external), and spanning capabilities. Inside-out capabilities refer to a company's internal resources and capabilities, which can be observed in aspects such as manufacturing, logistics, and human resource management. Outside-in capabilities are a company's capability to sense and respond to market changes and to develop and build relationships with customers. Spanning capabilities are the capabilities of companies to integrate inside-out and outside-in capabilities, which may encompass activities such as strategy development, pricing, product development, and procurement.

As we mentioned in the earlier chapters, operand resources are resources that must be acted upon to be beneficial and are usually finite and in tangible and static forms. On the other hand, operant resources act upon other resources to create benefits such as knowledge, skills, and capabilities. Operant resources are typically dynamic and invisible, and usually require a longer period of collective effort before results can be seen. Generally speaking, if a customer hopes to acquire operand resources, its outsourcing relationship with the service providers tends to be more transaction-driven and has a stronger emphasis on service efficiency. In contrast, if a customer places a stronger emphasis on gaining operant resources, it is more likely for the customer to build a stable partnership with the service provider, and the relationship pays more attention to effectiveness.

Danneels (2002) further introduced a new dimension to examine the level of interactions between different resources in a service offering and classified resources into two types: composite resources and interconnected resources. Composite resources are a simple combination of two or more basic resources that are owned by different service systems, and there is little interaction among the constituent basic resources, and the combination does not bring synergy. A simple example is the bundle of warehousing, logistics, and distribution in a logistics service menu. On the other hand, interconnected resources are a dynamic combination of resources that create synergy. There is a stronger degree of interactions among the constituent resources. An example would be the bundling of customs clearance, information services, cost management, warehousing, and transportation in a logistics service menu that brings great value for customers.

Given the types of resources (operand/operant) as well as the level of their interactions in service offering, we can classify the resources and capabilities acquired by customers in service outsourcing into four types: composite operand resources, composite operant resources, interconnected operand resources, and interconnected operant resources (Exhibit 5.3).

Exhibit 5.3: Different Types of Resources and Capabilities Acquired by Customers in Service Outsourcing

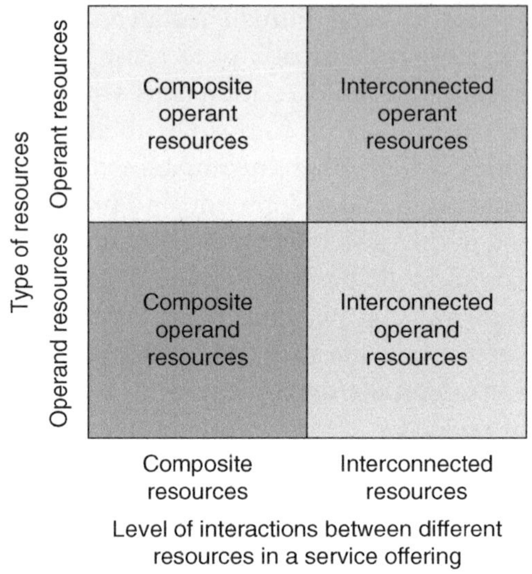

Four Types of Service Outsourcing: Perspective of Service Buyers

Taking into consideration the different types of resources and capabilities acquired in service outsourcing, from the perspective of service buyers, there are four types of service outsourcing: dispersed service outsourcing, cluster service outsourcing, in-sourcing service, and vested outsourcing (Exhibit 5.4).

Dispersed service outsourcing

In dispersed service outsourcing, service buyers and providers form loose relationships. Service buyers can change their service providers whenever they want. In this type of service outsourcing, service buyers mainly acquire composite operand resources, say, the outsourcing of logistics distribution and warehousing activities to third-party logistics providers. Although these activities are important to service buyers, they do not create much added value and synergy for businesses. Whether service providers can utilize their resources to offer the services efficiently at a low cost is the main concern of service buyers. In other words, in managing the outsourcing activities, service buyers focus mainly on behavior control of the service providers, that is,

Exhibit 5.4: Four Types of Service Outsourcing: Perspective of Service Buyers

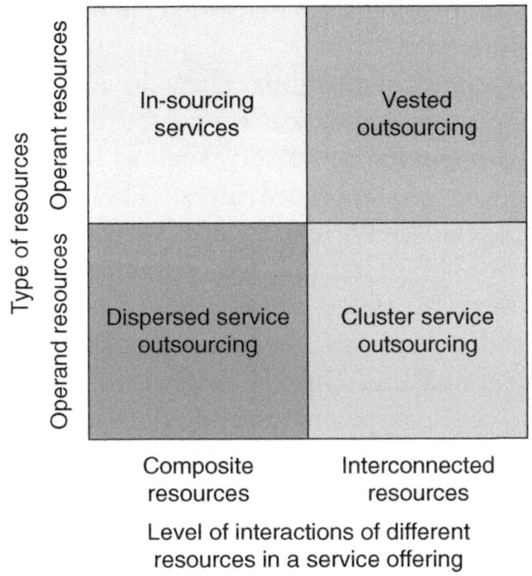

whether the service provisions by providers can meet their standards and expectations, and that quality services are delivered in a consistent manner and at low prices.

As composite operand resources can easily be measured, management of the service outsourcing tends to be contract-centered, instead of being relationship-centered. Service buyers tend to use contracts to state in detail the service specifications and requirements. Service providers must offer their services according to contracts; effective execution forms the basis for any further cooperation.

Cluster service outsourcing

Cluster service outsourcing means that in the acquisition of basic interconnected operand resources (or sometimes part of the operant resources), service providers not only pay attention to the capability of the service providers, but also place heavy emphasis on whether the services are provided in industry clusters. Cluster service outsourcing relies on service providers in industry clusters to supply interconnected operand resources and some of the operant resources. For instance, in the outsourcing of software design, development, and project management, service buyers are more focused on whether the location of the service provision enjoys industry cluster advantages. In recent years, cluster service outsourcing has been gaining attention.

In fact, the development of industry clusters has drawn the attention of economists as well as sociologists. The United Nations Industrial Development Organization defines "clusters as agglomerations of interconnected companies and associated institutions. Firms in a cluster produce similar or related goods or services and are supported by a range of dedicated institutions located in spatial proximity, such as business associations or training and technical assistance providers." The importance of clusters has also been highlighted by Porter. Porter (1998) defined clusters as "geographic concentrations of interconnected companies, specialized suppliers, service providers, firms in related industries, and associated institutions in particular fields that compete but also cooperate." DeWitt, Giunipero, and Melton (2006) suggested that clusters demonstrate three characteristics: physical proximity, core competencies, and relationships.

Clusters support companies in a number of ways, such as product development, production process improvement, technology, and marketing information (Tambunan, 2005). Birkinshaw and Hood (2000) empirically demonstrated that clustered companies enjoy much stronger supplier-customer bonds, government support, and decision-making autonomy than non-clustered companies. Porter (1998) explains how clusters affect competition in three ways: by raising the productivity of companies based in the area; by driving the direction and pace of innovation; and by stimulating the formation of new businesses within the cluster. From different studies on clusters, we can conclude that because of geographical proximity and more frequent transactions of clustered companies, clusters create an environment that fosters communication, coordination, interdependence, and trust for businesses based in the area, and this helps lower transaction costs and facilitates cooperation between upstream and downstream players. Companies in clusters benefit from network-based effects, particularly from enhanced social interactions (Harrison 1992).

Clusters create a more transparent environment that enables interconnected operand resources to come into full play. Unlike composite operand resources that companies can easily exercise control upon, interconnected operand resources are often complementary to one another—an open and transparent environment to allow effective and dynamic interactions of constituent resources are critical to create synergy, so that companies can lower system-wide transaction costs. This explains why practitioners tend to be more willing to outsource production operations to countries such as China and Mexico, but generally hold a more cautious attitude toward service outsourcing to these countries. According to a research study by Gartner, an information technology research and advisory company, 50% of all outsourcing contracts failed to meet expectations. Another study by global management consulting company PA Consulting Group suggested that only 39% of the interviewed companies extended their outsourcing contracts; 66% of companies were dissatisfied with the outsourcing projects, of which 15% had terminated their outsourcing contracts.

Major reasons behind the reluctance in service outsourcing include failure in compliance, cultural differences, and difficulty in supplier integration. In the past, off-shoring was very popular within the global outsourcing industry; the primary goal of service users was to lower costs. However, near-shoring has emerged as a growing trend since 2008. Apart from cost reduction, more and more service users prefer that their outsourced service providers be located in the same cluster, so as to achieve better synergy. The rise of Mexico as the top choice for manufacturing near-shoring of US companies is a case in point. Outsourcing to Mexico offers a number of advantages for US companies. First, the proximity to the United States—it takes between two and four hours of flight travel from various US locations to Mexico; US companies can enjoy huge cost savings working with Mexican service providers. Second, Mexico and the United States are in the same time zone. US companies can communicate easily with their Mexican service providers and grasp the latest developments in businesses. Third, compared with other countries, the American influence on Mexican culture facilitates communications between the service users and providers. Fourth, the Mexican government is highly supportive toward IT outsourcing in the country. With a series of government incentives such as Prosoft (Mexico's software industry development initiative), the number of IT companies in Mexico has climbed from 200 to 2,095. The Mexican government announced in 2011 that it would allocate 24 million pesos (about 240 million US dollars) to promote the IT industry developments in the country. It is hoped that the IT industry output will reach USD 150 billion by 2013.

Apart from using contracts to manage service providers, cluster service outsourcing tends to be more relationship-centered, that is, as mentioned by Gulati (1999), the parties place more emphasis on the length and quality of cooperation and customer satisfaction and these attributes form the basis for any further cooperation. The focus on relationships can be reflected in the investments in relationship-specific assets, which refers to the specific investments made by suppliers to implement customization for their buyers (Asanuma 1989; Levinthal and Fichman 1988). Wernerfelt (1988) referred to relationship-specific assets as resources developed by both service users and providers for shared use in long-term business relationships. Empirical studies by Zaheer and Venkatraman (1995) proved that relationship-specific investments foster a long-term relationship between companies and help eliminate opportunistic behaviour.

In-sourcing service

As opposed to outsourcing, in-sourcing is the practice of subcontracting work to another party, which is internal, and yet not a part of the organization. In *The World is Flat*, Friedman (2005) used UPS as a primary example for in-sourcing. Toshiba computers are repaired at the UPS hub by UPS employees, on behalf of Toshiba. Indeed, the disadvantages of the outsourcing model have prompted some companies to consider in-sourcing; the disadvantages include customer dissatisfaction, threat to security and confidentiality, quality problems due to lower costs, and changes in government policy that eliminate the low cost advantage of the service providers (Schniederjans, Schniederjans, and Schniederjans 2005). These problems are the most prominent in service users' acquisition of intangible operant resources. Clemons and Hitt (1997) brought to attention the problem of bounded contractibility, which leads to increases in transaction costs. Bounded contractibility chiefly says that it is not always easy to anticipate different issues in outsourcing as not all behavior can be measured and specified in an enforceable contract. Bounded contractibility may be due to limited foresight (the impossibility to anticipate all possible future conditions), limited observability (not all behaviours of interest are observable, or unambiguously verifiable), and cognitive limitations. In-sourcing, on the other hand, allows the service users to have better control over the value chains, internally integrate with service providers more effectively, and avoid increases in indirect or transactional costs due to external uncertainties.

The in-sourcing of the logistics operations of Nike China to LF Logistics in 2011 is a typical example of service supply chain in-sourcing. In February 2011, Nike announced the opening of its largest distribution center in Asia, the China Logistics Center in Taicang, Jiangsu. The distribution center covers an area of 460 *mus* with a building area of 200,000 square meters. The center has two parts—the first part is used for receiving, storage, sorting, and delivery; the other part is used for the storage and distribution of its footwear products. LF Logistics is responsible for the logistics operations of all Nike apparel, footwear, sports gear, and golf products in China. A driver of the cooperation with LF Logistics is that Nike considers the speed of order processing as the key to its success in China. Indeed, the company set an ambitious target of doubling its sales revenue from RMB 10 billion in 2011 to RMB 20 billion in 2015. However, the problem of lost sales due to poor order fulfilment is a dampener for many sports companies in China, including Nike. Apart from its self-operated stores, Nike also sells its footwear through some established distributors in China, such as Belle; but often, customers cannot find the Nike shoes they want in Belle stores due to poor fulfilment. As such, Nike built its distribution center in Taicang in a bid to shorten the distribution time and streamline the overall logistics operations with new technology applications.

Understanding successful modern logistics operations such as the use of warehousing management system (WMS), radio-frequency identification (RFID), voice recognition system, and so on requires a great deal of technical knowledge and management capabilities. Nike hopes to leverage on the knowledge and capabilities of an advanced third-party service provider instead of carrying out all the processes in-house. However, as logistics operations and other relevant order processing activities such as labeling are of strategic importance to the sales operations of Nike, the company wants to have better control over these activities and therefore, logistics outsourcing is not an option. Eventually, LF Logistics was chosen as exclusive service provider for Nike; LF Logistics would offer to Nike a comprehensive range of logistics and management services in the Taicang distribution center. All asset investments in the distribution center were made by Nike. The in-sourcing arrangements helped enhance its logistics performance in China; at the same time, Nike is freed from the burden of non-core logistics operations in China and can focus on product development and sales.

In-sourcing service users tend to pay better attention to operand resources; therefore, apart from using contracts to manage service providers, managing in-sourcing service tends to be more relationship-centered. This can be reflected in the investments in human capital- and knowledge-driven relationship-specific assets. Besides, in-sourcing relationships are built on a high level of trust.

Vested outsourcing

Vested outsourcing is a concept introduced by Vitasek and Ledyard in the article *Vested Outsourcing: A Better Way to Outsource* in *Harvard Business Review* in 2009. Later in August 2010, Vitasek and Ledyard discussed the concept again in the article *Vested Outsourcing: Game-Changing Rules for Outsourcing* in *Globalization Today*. Vitasek and Ledyard (2009, 2010) pointed out that the traditional descriptions of outsourcing have described three types of relationships: (1) transactional (where a certain distance is maintained from the service provider, with a unit price and a purchase order for each service), (2) preferred supplier (where a supplier is prequalified and there may be a long-term agreement; a blanket purchase order is used), and (3) strategic alliance (which is characterized by a high-level relationship between the buyer and service provider, with shared intelligence and operational tie-ins. Vested outsourcing, as Vitasek and Ledyard (ibid.) have claimed, is a

> fundamental business model paradigm shift in how a company and its outsourcing service providers conduct business. It creates a new level between the preferred supplier and strategic alliance...The heart of the vested outsourcing contract is an agreement on desired outcomes, which explicitly states the results on which both companies will base their contract. The vested outsourcing agreement defines financial rewards or penalties for exceeding or not meeting the desired outcomes. Vested outsourcing is not gainsharing. The service provider is challenged to provide brainpower and/or investments to solve the buyer's problem. Providers may also take on risks to accomplish this, in essence, putting 'skin in the game'.

The result is a win-win vested outsourcing partnership." Vitasek and Ledyard suggested that "vested outsourcing is more focused than a strategic alliance, and does not require as much operational infrastructure. But it takes the preferred supplier relationship to a whole new level."

Vitasek and Ledyard (ibid.) suggested that Microsoft and Intel, both well-known for their innovative cultures, are early advocates for vested outsourcing. Microsoft has successfully adopted this model for its facilities management and accounting, and was awarded for its cooperation with Accenture, in which the latter manages Microsoft's back office procure-to-pay process. However, adopting the new model is challenging for many businesses. Vitasek and Ledyard (ibid.) quoted the advice by Tim McBride, CPO, for Microsoft: "We have learned that applying a vested outsourcing philosophy requires a cultural change in how we will need to work with our suppliers. For Microsoft, this means exploring vested outsourcing one program and one supplier at a time—working to build trust with our supply base and business units that outsource to understand that there really is a better way." Although no vested outsourcing relationships are the same, they are all based on common causes of boosting innovation, optimizing services, lowering the costs for service users, as well as enhancing the profits of service providers. Vested outsourcing is more effective than rewarding excellent services solely by giving bonuses.

The basic principle of vested outsourcing is to encourage service providers to proactively explore different means such as operations improvements, new technology, and capabilities to benefit their customers. Unlike traditional outsourcing where service providers get paid to perform a designated business activity, in a vested outsourcing relationship, service providers are paid to solve problems for their service users. This means that service providers are challenged to input intelligence or capital to solve their customers' problems, and furthermore, they have the risks transferred to themselves when promising greater value creation for their customers. In exchange, service users allow their service providers to reap bigger profit potentials than industry average to achieve ever-increasing value creation. Service users and providers develop performance-based solutions such that interests of both sides are aligned, and they are essentially vested in each others' success. Vested outsourcing is a win-win partnership. Unlike different types of outsourcing, vested outsourcing focuses its attention on interconnected operant resources. It highlights the importance of knowledge and innovation to realize mutual benefits.

Vested outsourcing calls for a change in management mindsets. Although the importance of partnership is widely recognized in traditional outsourcing, companies optimize partnerships for their own self-interests. The self-interests-come-first attitude is reflected in "What's in it for me?" (the WIIFMe mentality). Vested outsourcing, on the other hand, concerns "What's in it for we?" (the WIIFWe mentality). Vested outsourcing seeks to unlock a greater system-wide opportunity, instead of maximizing the benefits of a single side. Obviously, this requires the commitment and efforts of both sides. Service users should not think of themselves being exempt from the outsourced activities; on the contrary, they have to communicate with their service providers on a regular and frequent basis to set new targets and manage the work. The true WIIFWE mentality is new to many companies; both service providers and users have to learn to operate under this new philosophy.

Human relationships play a crucial role in successful vested outsourcing. In a vested outsourcing relationship, both service providers and users work together upon mutual trusts, and both are responsible for achieving the outcomes. There are five major rules to build a win-win vested outsourcing relationship.

Rule 1: Focus on outcomes, not transactions

Many traditional outsourcing arrangements are transaction based. Most of the time, this model uses a cost-plus or a competitively bid fixed-price-per-transaction pricing model to ensure that the service buyers get the lowest cost per transaction. This could mean that the more inefficient the business process, the more profitable the service provider. Vested outsourcing, on the other hand, is outcome-based. The service providers are paid after achieving the desired outcomes. With the interests of both sides aligned, vested outsourcing offers more efficient solutions at lower costs.

Rule 2: Service users focus on the WHAT, not the HOW

In vested outsourcing relationships, service users purchase their services differently. Instead of designating how service providers should offer support to their businesses, service users specify what their goals are and shift the responsibility of determining how the services should be delivered to the service provider. The rationale behind this is that service providers outsource business activities that they are less capable of handling, and leave it to the service providers to use their expertise and decide how to get things done to yield better results.

Rule 3: Agree on clearly defined and measurable outcomes

In a vested outsourcing relationship, both service users and providers agree on clearly defined and measurable desired outcomes. Both sides should spend time together during the outsourcing process, and in particular, during contract negotiations, to establish explicit definitions for how the desired outcomes will be measured. The service provider can propose a pricing model that specifies the required level of performance at a predetermined price. Under vested outsourcing, service providers are paid for the value they deliver, instead of the activities performed.

Rule 4: Optimize pricing model incentives for cost/service trade-offs

Vested outsourcing relationship adopts a pricing model that incorporates incentives for the most optimal cost and service trade-off. When establishing the pricing model, there are two principles: (1) risk and reward for both service users and providers must be balanced and (2) it must specify that service providers will deliver solutions, not just business activities.

Vested outsourcing does not guarantee higher profits for service providers, but it grants service providers the discretionary power to make strategic investments in service processes that may generate greater returns on investment.

Rule 5: Governance structure provides insight, not merely oversight

In traditional outsourcing, some service users simply outsource their activities to service providers with poorly defined requirements and often without any performance metrics or service level agreements. Some service users, on the other hand, have gone to another extreme and require service providers to be strict rule followers. Vested outsourcing relationships see service providers as real experts in the outsourced area. Therefore, the governance structure highlights the importance of good communications rather than supervision, to exchange insight.

Chapter 6

Business Model Innovation—The Service Supply Chain Strategy of Li & Fung

For both new and established companies, having a suitable business model is crucial for success. Business models determine several important factors including the scope of business activities, competitive positioning, profit levels, and relevant resources and capabilities required, and have practical implications on areas such as pricing. However, because of changes in the business environment, companies must periodically review and, if necessary, transform their business models. Often, business model transformation is not easy because of inertia and resistance to change. In this chapter, we will use the business model transformation of Li & Fung as an example to see how companies adapt to changes with service supply chain initiatives. As discussed in Chapter 2, the concept of service supply chains is continually evolving. We hope the business model innovation case study of Li & Fung will further readers' understanding of service supply chain practices.

Business Model Transformation

There are many different definitions of business models. Afuah and Tucci (2000) viewed business models as a system of components (value, revenue sources, prices, related activities, implementation, capabilities, and sustainability), relationships, and interrelated technology; in other words, business models are dynamic. Johnson et al. (2008) suggested that business models should include key processes such as training, development, manufacturing, budgeting, planning, sales, and service. Mitchell and Coles (2003) described business models as the combination of "who," "what," "when," "where," "why," and "how" a company provides its customers with its products and services. Eisenmann (2002) stated that a business model is a model of the business activities of a company enabling it to serve its customers. Chesbrough and Rosenbloom (2002), on the other hand, suggested that a business model defines the structure of the value chain within a company required to create and distribute the offerings to customers. It involves a series of activities, from raw materials sourcing to satisfying the end consumers, which will yield a new product or service in a way that net value is created throughout the process.

The creation of every business model has its own antecedents and will bring new consequences; business model transformation usually corresponds to new changes in environment (Magretta 2002). Similarly, N. Siggelkow (2001, 2002) pointed out that business model transformation often implies changes in the competitive environment of a company. Let us follow this line of thought to explore the business transformation and innovation of the Li & Fung Group.

Exhibit 6.1: Transformation of a Business Model

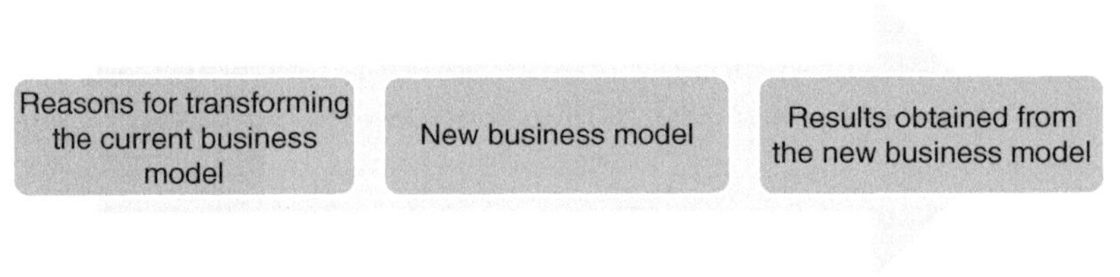

Li & Fung Group

The Li & Fung Group is a multinational company headquartered in Hong Kong with three core businesses: trading, logistics and distribution, and retailing (Exhibit 6.2). Li & Fung operates its business along the lines of the supply chain management philosophy. With over 105 years of work history, Li & Fung was among the first group of Chinese companies that engaged in foreign trade in the country. Today, Li & Fung is recognized as the world leader in consumer goods design, development, sourcing, and distribution. With over 34,000 employees in more than 240 offices and distribution centers in over 40 economies spanning across America, Europe, Africa, and Asia, Li & Fung manages the supply chain for retailers and brands worldwide. The company recorded a total revenue of USD 21 billion in 2011.

Exhibit 6.2: Group Structure of Li & Fung

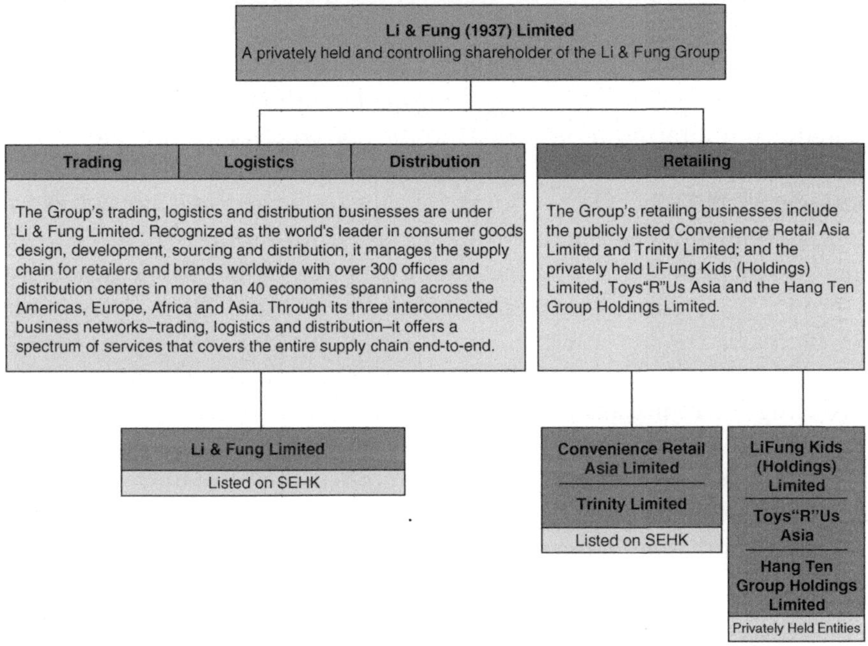

The trading business, which is listed in the Hong Kong Stock Exchange as Li & Fung Limited (0494.HK), accounts for approximately 70%–80% of the revenue of the Li & Fung Group. Li & Fung Limited helps retailers across the world source a wide range of consumer products that can be categorized as: (1) soft goods, that is, apparel; (2) hard goods, that is, non-apparel products such as toys, home furnishings, sporting goods, and footwear; and (3) health, beauty, and cosmetics (HBC). Soft goods contribute to approximately 70% of the revenue of the trading arm. Li & Fung entered the HBC category in 2007; today, the HBC category has 1%–2% share of the total revenue. The second core business is logistics distribution, which was formerly conducted by IDS. In 2010, Li & Fung Limited privatized IDS to make the latter its wholly owned subsidiary. The third core business is retailing, which includes publicly listed luxury menswear retailer Trinity Limited and convenience store operator Convenience Retail Asia, as well as the privately held Toys (Lauban) Holding Limited, which is licensed to operate Toys"R"Us stores.

In this book, we limit our discussion to the business transformation of Li & Fung Limited. As you will see, Li & Fung has expanded its scope of services through the years.

Business Model Transformation of Li & Fung

The Li & Fung Group was founded in Guangzhou, China, by Fung Pak-liu in 1906, the grandfather of Victor Fung, the present Group Chairman of Li & Fung Group. It was among the first Chinese-owned export trading companies in China. In the early days, the business scope of the company was simple. Fung Pak-liu leveraged on his English language capabilities to facilitate communication between buyers and sellers, and charged 15% of the turnover of successfully "matched" businesses as commissions. Strictly speaking, Li & Fung was a trading intermediary then and not an export trading company. The operation mode lasted for around 70 years. When Fung Pak-liu passed on the business to Victor Fung's father, Li & Fung derived its profits from commissions coordinating buyer and seller transactions. However, as a trading intermediary, Li & Fung faced challenges posed by the growing power of buyers and factories. The competitive pressure pushed Li & Fung's commission rate down to 10%, then 5%, and even 3%. The business model transformation and innovation of Li & Fung began in 1976, when Victor Fung and William Fung returned to Hong Kong upon completion of their studies in the United States and joined the company.

Li & Fung has undergone five major business model transformations since the 70s:

First transformation (mid 1970s–early 1980s)

Li & Fung transformed from a purchasing agent to a regional purchasing company. The company expanded and established offices in different parts of Asia, such as China, Taiwan, Korea, and Singapore. Apart from providing the latest market information to buyers, service offerings of Li & Fung also extended to include factory evaluation (e.g., product quality and productivity), vendor selection, price negotiation, and quality management for buyers so that they could source at more reasonable prices. On the other hand, Li & Fung also assisted factories in production management, and helped buyers monitor factory compliance in various areas such as labor regulation, production environment, and environment protection to ensure that international standards were met. All in all, as a purchasing company, Li & Fung aimed to help develop long-term win-win partnership between factories and buyers. With the introduction of a new business and management concept, Li & Fung moved to the next level (Exhibit 6.3).

Second transformation (early 1980s–late 1980s)

Li & Fung made the transition into a borderless manufacturing planning and management company in the 1980s amid rising costs in Hong Kong and intensifying market competition from other rising Asian companies. While the traditional sourcing model was that a customer requested a specific

Exhibit 6.3: Transformation from a Purchasing Agent to a Regional Purchasing Company

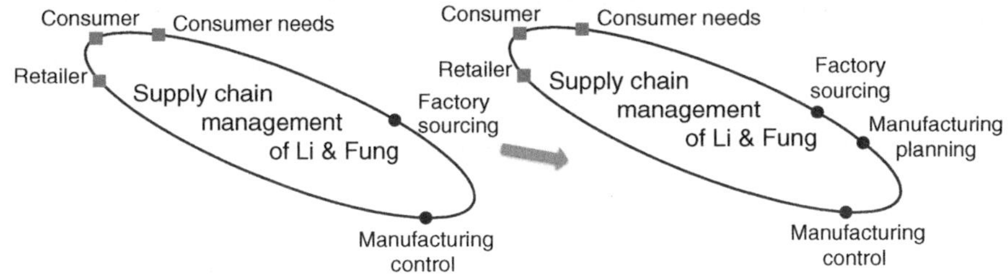

product and Li & Fung found the best supplier, borderless manufacturing chiefly meant that the company performed production slicing to identify the best location to undertake each stage of the production process, and the final products would be assembled from components sourced from many countries. Once its customer had an idea of the products, it would send the design sketches to Li & Fung. Based on customer requirements such as design, colors, quality, and comments from its design team, Li & Fung carried out market research and located the best suppliers for components such as fabrics and yarn from different places, and developed a complete production plan. Li & Fung monitored the entire process to ensure product quality and on-time delivery.

Li & Fung became an expert at finding the best solution for each step in the manufacturing process. It performed high value-added business operations such as design and quality control in Hong Kong and moved lower value-added operations such as production to other lower-cost countries such as China. Manufacturing process became truly globalized (Exhibit 6.4).

Exhibit 6.4: Transformation from a Regional Purchasing Company to a Borderless Manufacturing Planning and Management Company

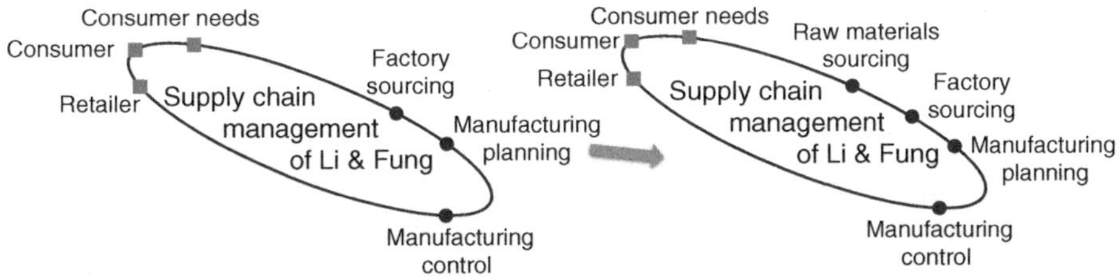

Third transformation (early 1990s–early 2000s)

Borderless manufacturing practices in the 1980s brought new challenges. Dispersed manufacturing prompted the company to break the value chains and allocate different value-added activities to the best possible locations across the world. The company was no longer an intermediary or agent; it became the supplier for its customers. Li & Fung would sign contracts with overseas buyers directly and planned, managed, and monitored the entire production process from product design, sourcing, production management, and control as well as other auxiliary activities such as logistics and forwarding consolidation. As before, Li & Fung did not own any factories; it outsourced production tasks to different factories (Exhibit 6.5).

Exhibit 6.5: Transformation from a Borderless Manufacturing Planning and Management Company to a Virtual Manufacturer

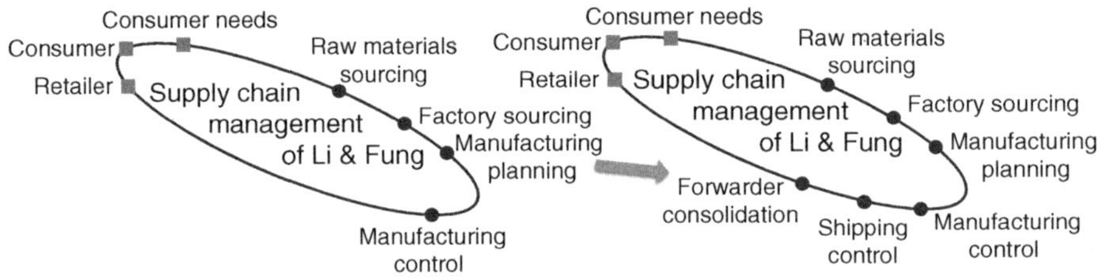

Fourth transformation (early 2000s–2010)

From a virtual manufacturer managing the entire supply chain for its customers, Li & Fung further transformed itself to become a network orchestrator to enhance flexibility and responsiveness. A network can be understood as a robust universe of suppliers from which different supply chains can be drawn. Indeed, network orchestration concerns developing and managing the network, and effectively designing and managing supply chains according to specific customer requirements. Each supply chain is unique; the supply chains of the same products from the same customer can differ due to differences in requested lead time. Li & Fung had a growing network of 15,000 suppliers (Exhibit 6.6).

Li & Fung orchestrates not only the sourcing network but also the logistics and distribution networks for its customers, bringing them the most effective supply chain solutions and cost-competitive products.

Exhibit 6.6: Network and Supply Chains

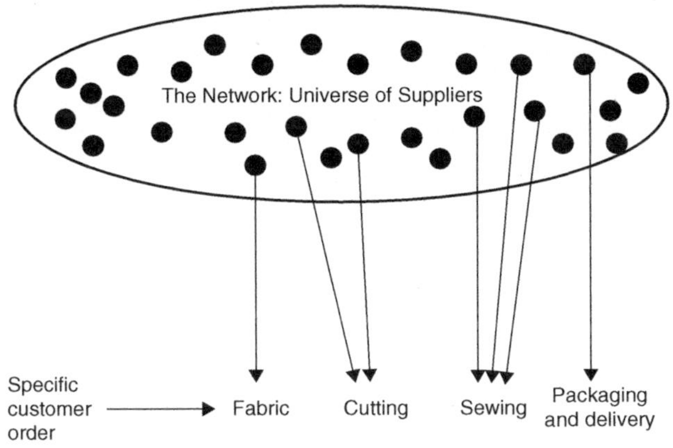

The fifth transformation (2010–present)

Li & Fung went on to become an integrated supply chain solutions provider (a service supply chain operator). From product design, raw material sourcing, production, logistics and onshore distribution, it can be said that Li & Fung manages an entire service supply chain for its customers (Exhibit 6.7). For instance, in managing the supply chains for the retail giant Wal-Mart, Li & Fung monitors every single process such as raw material sourcing, manufacturing, packaging, quality control, and measuring the carbon footprints of the Wal-Mart supply chain.

Exhibit 6.7: From a Network Orchestrator to an Integrated Supply Chain Solutions Provider

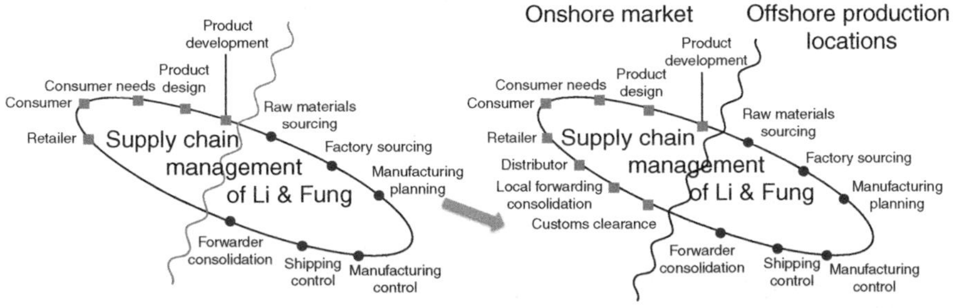

To provide end-to-end solutions to customers, Li & Fung orchestrates the sourcing network, logistics network, and onshore distribution network (Exhibit 6.8).

Exhibit 6.8: Three Networks Managed by Li & Fung

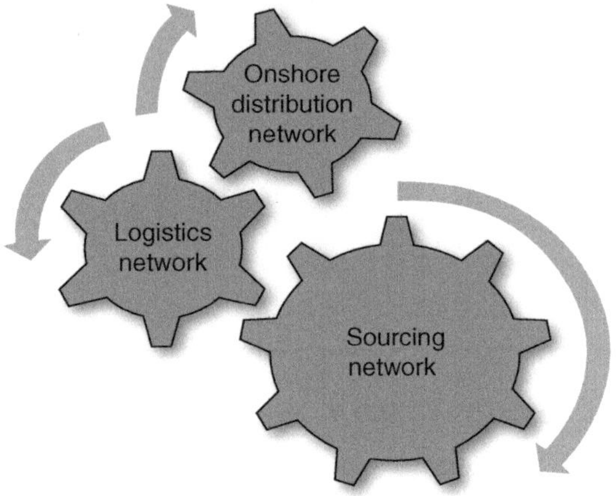

First among these is the traditional sourcing network. Li & Fung has 62 sourcing offices worldwide. Of these, around 40% are located in China, and the others are located in larger sourcing markets such as Vietnam, Bangladesh, Indonesia, and in Central European countries such as Turkey, Bulgaria, and Egypt. Customers choose to source from Li & Fung not because of its price competitiveness, but because of its strong capabilities in design, management of entire production flow, and quality control. Li & Fung's global network of suppliers also boosts its market responsiveness. For instance, when the Severe Acute Respiratory Syndrome (SARS) struck southern China, Li & Fung quickly switched production from the above-mentioned areas to countries such as Vietnam, Indonesia, and Bangladesh, thereby minimizing disruptions in supply chains.

The second network is the logistics network. Li & Fung strengthened its logistics network after the privatization of IDS, which has 30 logistics offices and 96 warehouses and distribution centers across the globe. Li & Fung's logistics businesses are very strong in China and other Southeast Asian countries such as Malaysia, Thailand, and Singapore. As per its latest three-year plan (2011–2013), Li & Fung aims to expand its logistics businesses in Europe and the United States, which are comparatively less mature.

Finally, the third network is the onshore distribution network. Li & Fung currently has 48 onshore distribution offices worldwide, which engage in wholesale distribution businesses. Li & Fung has a particularly strong wholesale distribution network in the United States; the company has developed close relationships with renowned retailers such as Macy's and Kohl's. Through brand licensing, Li & Fung sells products to different format retailers such as department stores and specialty stores. Today, there are over 300 licensed brands in Li & Fung's portfolio. A recent example of its onshore distribution business is the launch of the Jennifer Lopez collection in the US market.

All in all, the business model evolution of Li & Fung can be summarized as below (Exhibit 6.9). It is noteworthy that each transformation is not a radical change to the previous model, but building on service add-ons and innovations.

Exhibit 6.9: The Evolution of Li & Fung's Business Model

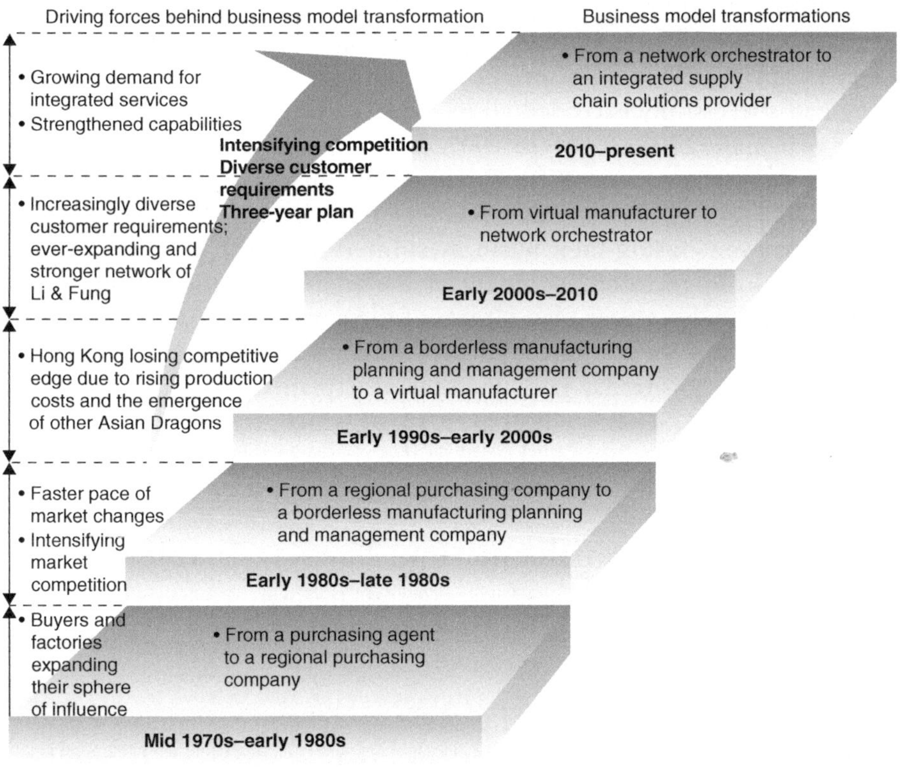

It is evident that intensifying competition and increasingly diverse customer requirements drive business model transformation. We will now also study why the three-year plan of Li & Fung serves as one of the driving forces behind its business model transformation.

Li & Fung regards its three-year plan as a successful way to ensure continuous improvements. Its three-year plan was actually inspired by China's "Five-year Plan," which is a series of social and economic development initiatives made every five years that guide the country's direction of developments. Once the plan is announced, the whole nation focuses on reaching the targets. Taking into account the rapid pace of market changes in the business world, companies need to balance stability and renewal; Li & Fung thus draws up its company plan every three years. The goals in the plan would stay the same throughout the three-year period.

More important, Li & Fung adopts a zero-based approach in setting its three-year plan, that is, it starts from ground zero, by asking the important question: "Assuming we didn't have our business today, would we go into it?" Stretched objectives result not only in business model transformation, but also force executives to think outside the box, driving innovation and breakthroughs.

2011 marked a new start for the 8th three-year plan (2011–2013) of Li & Fung. Up until the last seven three-year plans of Li & Fung, the company had successfully exceeded all its targets, except in the case of its 7th three-year plan (2008–2010). In 2007, Li & Fung set a USD 1 billion core operating profit target by 2010. However, the financial crisis in 2008 and 2009 dealt a serious blow to many retailers in the United States and Europe, with some even closing their businesses. Interviews with executives in the Li & Fung Group revealed that financial market headwinds did not result in a change in the three-year plan targets of the company; Li & Fung worked harder to expand its customer base and strengthen service offerings, and mergers and acquisitions. The 8th three-year plan targets core operating profits, reaching USD 1.5 billion by 2013; of which, trading, logistics, and distribution will contribute USD 700 million, 100 million, and 700 million, respectively.

Business Model Transformation: The Key Enablers

Li & Fung has sought to build its capacity through a number of ways, such as mergers and acquisitions (M&As), human resources training, and information technology.

Mergers and acquisitions (M & As)

In the past 15 years, Li & Fung has embarked on 45 M&As. In 2010, the company carried out 12 M&As, one of which was a domestic company in

China and the remaining were companies in the United States and Europe. Li & Fung has a targeted M&As strategy—instead of seeking immediate investment returns, the company aims to locate investment opportunities that support business growth. Li & Fung uses M&As to fill the gap in its business coverage, and terms it as "filling in the mosaic." For instance, the company has built a presence and know-how in the jeans segment through acquiring players in the field.

Human resource training

Solid understanding of the products and different supply chain processes is a prerequisite for strong service provisions. Li & Fung has taken a series of human resource training and knowledge management initiatives. Aside from offering technical training to merchandisers, Li & Fung also spends a large amount of resources to develop training programs for its management staff. For example, the Li & Fung Leadership Program, which was targeted toward its senior managers, was launched in collaboration with the Massachusetts Institute of Technology (MIT) Sloan School of Management and the University of Hong Kong in 2010. Li & Fung also pays huge attention to the training of designers. Currently, the company has around 400 designers in New York and London, and a designer team in Asia. Li & Fung offers training programs to their designers in Hong Kong, New York, and Paris.

Li & Fung has over 200 independent business divisions. To facilitate internal knowledge sharing, the company holds internal global conferences at least twice a year for its senior managers and customers to facilitate the exchange of experiences and ideas. The company also organizes sharing sessions, lectures, and seminars internally on a regular basis. Besides, the company has an internal knowledge management platform that uses the Microsoft SharePoint system to promote internal discussions.

The Li & Fung staff participate actively in various trade shows to keep abreast with latest market developments. Furthermore, the company also subscribes to the services of different business intelligence service providers.

Information technology

To lower costs and minimise lead time, Li & Fung invests huge sums of money in its information technology systems to ensure unimpeded information and physical flows, both internally and externally with suppliers and customers. For instance, Import Direct is a core e-commerce system powered by Li & Fung that targets its hard goods customers. It is a useful promotion platform for suppliers, whereby they can upload the images of their products to the product catalogues in the systems. It is also an excellent channel for sourcing and tracking processes for the customers of Li & Fung. Customers can search for relevant product information and place their orders in Import Direct.

Business Model Innovations: The Results

Over the years, Li & Fung has become a leading global supply chain management company of business model evolution. Today, the company has 34,000 employees and more than 240 offices and distribution centers in over 40 economies, plus access to a growing network of 15,000 suppliers. Let us take a look at the results achieved by the Li & Fung Group, from its major customers, major awards and recognitions, as well as its financial performance over the past 10 years.

Major customers of Li & Fung

Many of the major customers of Li & Fung are leading retailers in the United States and Europe. In addition, the customer base of Li & Fung is ever increasing. In February 2010, Li & Fung entered an agreement to supply clothes and other consumer goods to retail giant Wal-Mart, which Li & Fung management said could bring the company an "addressable business" of as much as USD 100 billion. In November 2011, the company became a sourcing agent for Li Ning, China's largest domestic sportswear company. The agreement covers sourcing for popular running, basketball, and lifestyle lines for Li Ning in both international and domestic markets.

Major awards and recognitions in recent years

Exhibit 6.10 highlights the major awards and recognitions of Li & Fung over the past six years.

Financial performance of Li & Fung in the past 10 years

As seen in Exhibits 6.11–6.13, except for the financial year of 2008, Li & Fung has enjoyed steady increase in turnover, operating profit and net profit over the 10 past years. Undoubtedly, the generally favorable market conditions over the past decade provided impetus for growth; but constant efforts by Li & Fung to explore new possibilities in business models and transform flexibly to respond to market changes also play a meaningful role.

Exhibit 6.10 Major Awards and Recognitions of Li & Fung, 2006–2010

Award	2005	2006	2007	2008	2009	2010
1	The Gold Award in the Hang Seng Index Category of the "Best Corporate Governance Disclosure Awards 2005" organized by the Hong Kong Institute of Certified Public Accountants	The Gold Award in the Hang Seng Index Category of the "Best Corporate Governance Disclosure Awards 2006" organized by the Hong Kong Institute of Certified Public Accountants	"Corporate Governance Asia Recognition Awards 2007" by *Corporate Governance Asia Journal*	"Corporate Governance Asia Recognition Awards 2008" by *Corporate Governance Asia Journal*	"Global 2000: The World's Biggest Public Companies" Ranked number 888 in Forbes; April 2009	Ranked No. 2 in Asia (ex-Japan) and Hong Kong large caps companies in corporate governance ranking surveyed by CLSA and ACGA in September 2010
2	Included in the "Top Quartile Companies" in Hong Kong with the highest corporate governance score surveyed by CLSA and Asian Corporate Governance Association	"Corporate Governance Asia Recognition Awards 2006" by *Corporate Governance Asia Journal*	"Hong Kong Best Managed Company—No. 1" and "Best Corporate Governance—No. 2" by *Finance Asia* magazine	"Fabulous 50" by Forbes Asia in September 2008	"FT Global 500 Companies" by *Financial Times* in September 2009	"Hong Kong Best Managed Company—No. 2" "Hong Kong Best Corporate Governance—No. 4" by *Finance Asia* magazine's poll

(*Continued*)

Exhibit 6.10 Major Awards and Recognitions of Li & Fung, 2006–2010 (*Continued*)

Award	2005	2006	2007	2008	2009	2010
3	"Highly Commended—Best Corporate Governance Awards 2005" by *Investor Relations* magazine	"Hong Kong Best Managed Company—No. 1" and "Best Corporate Governance—No. 2" by *Finance Asia* magazine	"The Asset Corporate Governance Awards 2007" by *The Asset* magazine	"The World's Most Influential Companies" by *Business Week* in December 2008	"The World's Best Companies—Top 40" by *Business Week* in October 2009	"Most convincing and coherent strategy—No. 3" and "Best corporate governance—No. 5" in Hong Kong by Euromoney's "Asia best-managed companies" poll in January 2010
4		"Asia's Best Managed Companies in Hong Kong 2006" by *Asia Money* magazine	"Fabulous 50" by Forbes Asia	"50 for 2012" Companies by Morgan Stanley in December 2008	"Fabulous 50" Companies by Forbes Asia in September 2009	"Asia's Best-Managed Companies 2010" Named Large-Cap Corporate of the Year, Hong Kong in *Asia Money's* awards in December 2010

5		Ranking among the top of Hong Kong public companies with the highest corporate governance score surveyed by the City University of Hong Kong (sponsored by the Hong Kong Institute of Directors)	Ranking among the Top 5 of Hong Kong large caps companies in corporate governance ranking surveyed by CLSA and ACGA survey	"The Asset Corporate Governance Awards 2008" by *The Asset* magazine	"Corporate Governance Asia Recognition Awards 2009" by *Corporate Governance Asia Journal*	"Corporate Governance Asia Recognition Awards 2010" and "1st Asian Corporate Director Recognition Awards 2010" to Dr. Victor Fung by *Corporate Governance Asia Journal* in 2010
6				"Hong Kong's Best Managed Company—No. 4" by *Finance Asia* survey in June 2008	"Asia's Best-Managed Companies 2009" named Large-Cap Corporate of the Year, Hong Kong in *Asia Money's* awards; December 2009	"Fabulous 50" Companies by Forbes Asia in December 2010

(*Continued*)

Exhibit 6.10 Major Awards and Recognitions of Li & Fung, 2006–2010 (*Continued*)

Award	2005	2006	2007	2008	2009	2010
7					"Long-term Vision—No. 4", "Innovation—No. 5", "Most-admired Company—No. 9" "Corporate Reputation—No. 9" in Hong Kong by *Wall Street Journal Asia*'s "200 Most-admired" Companies Survey" in September 2009	"The Asset Corporate Platinum Award 2010" For all round excellence in financial performance, corporate governance, management, social responsibility, environmental responsibility, and investor relations by *The Asset* magazine in December 2010

Source: 2010 annual report of Li & Fung.

Exhibit 6.11: Turnover of Li & Fung, 2001–2010

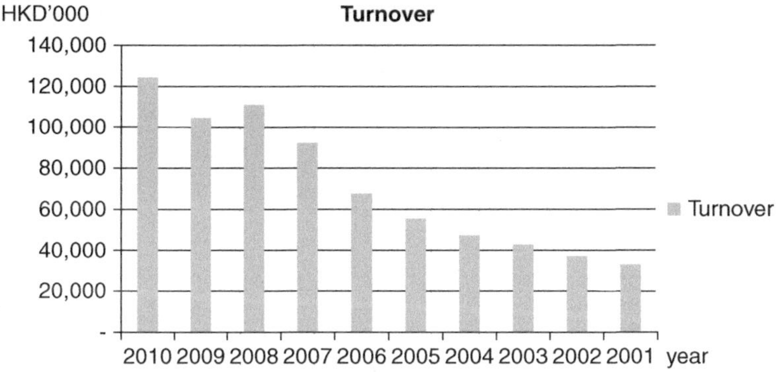

Source: Li & Fung Annual Report 2010.

Exhibit 6.12: Operating Profit of Li & Fung, 2001–2010

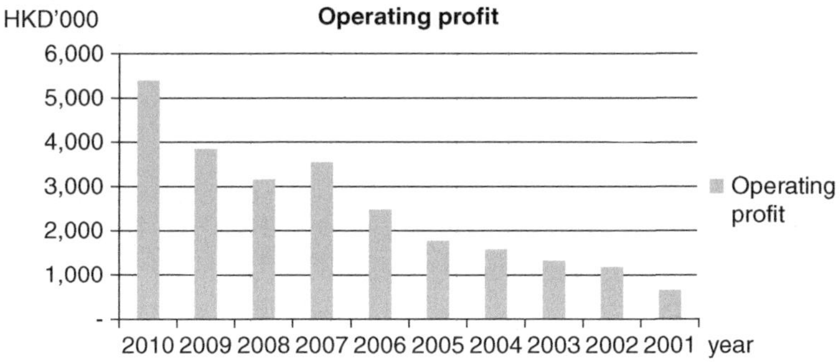

Source: Li & Fung Annual Report 2010.

Exhibit 6.13: Net Profit of Li & Fung, 2001–2010

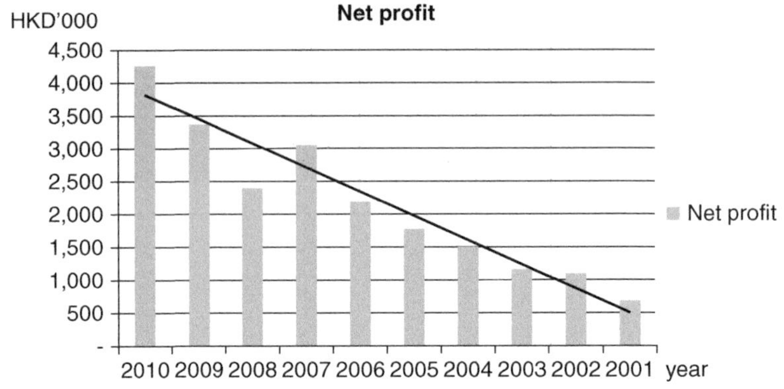

Source: Li & Fung Annual Report 2010.

Exhibit 6.14: Financial Summary of Li & Fung, 2001–2010

	2010 HK$'000	2009 HK$'000	2008 HK$'000	2007 HK$'000	2006 HK$'000	2005 HK$'000	2004 HK$'000	2003 HK$'000	2002 HK$'000	2001 HK$'000
Turnover										
Continuing operations	**124,115,167**	104,478,983	110,722,117	92,459,949	68,010,257	55,617,374	47,170,601	42,630,510	37,281,360	32,941,392
Discontinued operations	–	–	–	–	–	–	–	–	–	87,183
	124,115,167	104,478,983	110,722,117	92,459,949	68,010,257	55,617,374	47,170,601	42,630,510	37,281,360	33,028,575
Operating profit										
Continuing operations	**5,298,682**	3,879,506	3,044,416	3,600,053	2,412,320	1,884,600	1,556,036	1,251,986	1,137,025	906,940
Discontinued operations	–	–	–	–	–	–	–	–	–	(237,955)
	5,298,682	3,879,506	3,044,416	3,600,053	2,412,320	1,884,600	1,556,036	1,251,986	1,137,025	668,985
Interest income	**105,815**	90,763	112,748	208,193	98,491	69,539	43,163	38,373	49,581	112,837
Interest expenses	**(767,855)**	(372,109)	(480,175)	(499,664)	(148,070)	(21,376)	(11,466)	(9,813)	(8,967)	(12,464)
Share of profit less losses of associated companies	**14,431**	7,787	6,197	4,948	10,603	9,062	32,801	431	(1,683)	(345)
Profit before taxation	**4,651,073**	3,606,947	2,683,186	3,313,530	2,373,344	1,941,825	1,620,534	1,280,977	1,175,981	769,013
Taxation	**(370,698)**	(240,222)	(259,497)	(252,554)	(171,682)	(151,248)	(130,250)	(103,929)	(92,865)	(53,849)
Profit for the year	**4,280,375**	3,365,725	2,423,699	3,060,976	2,201,662	1,790,577	1,490,284	1,177,048	1,083,116	715,164
Attributable to:										
Continuing operations	**4,278,221**	3,369,107	2,421,936	3,060,036	2,201,819	1,790,279	1,491,223	1,189,152	1,082,888	953,727
Discontinued operations	–	–	–	–	–	–	–	–	–	(168,996)
Shareholders of the Company	**4,278,221**	3,369,107	2,421,936	3,060,036	2,201,819	1,790,279	1,491,223	1,189,152	1,082,888	784,731
Non-controlling interests	**2,154**	(3,382)	1,753	940	(157)	298	(939)	(12,104)	228	(69,567)
	4,280,375	3,365,725	2,423,689	3,060,976	2,201,662	1,790,577	1,490,284	1,177,048	1,083,116	715,164
Earnings per share (HK cents) *(Note)*										
Basic	**111.9**	91.0	69.3	89.5	67.1	55.6	46.5	37.4	34.1	24.8
Continuing operations	**111.9**	91.0	69.3	89.5	67.1	55.6	46.5	37.4	34.1	30.2
Dividend per share (HK cents) *(Note)*	**90**	75.0	57.0	71.0	55.0	45.5	38.2	31.8	27.7	24.1
Special dividend per share (HK cents) *(Note)*	–	–	–	–	–	–	22.7	–	–	–

Source: "Ten Year Financial Summary," *Li & Fung Annual Report 2011.*

Bibliography

Adenso-Diaz, B., P. González-Torre, and V. García. "A Capacity Management Model in Service Industries." *International Journal of Service Industry Management* 13 (2002): 71–9.

Afuah, A., and C. L. Tucci. "Internet Business Models and Strategies: Text and Cases." New York: Irwin/McGraw-Hill, 2000.

Asanuma, Banri. "The Contractual Framework for Parts Supply in the Japanese Automotive Industry." *Japanese Economic Studies* 12 (1985): 54–78.

Axelsson, B., and F. Wynstra. "Interaction Patterns in Services Exchange-Some Thoughts on the Impact of Different Kinds of Services in Buyer-supplier Interfaces and Interactions." 16th Annual IMP Conference. Bath, United Kingdom, 2000, 2002.

Axelssori, B. "Interaction Patterns in Services Exchange—Some Thoughts on the Impact of Different Kinds of Services on Buyer-Supplier Interfaces and Interactions." Working Paper, 16th IMP-conference in Bath, U. K., 2000.

Bain, Joe Staten. *Barriers to New Competition*. Cambridge: Harvard University Press, 1956.

Barney, Jay. "Firm Resources and Sustained Competitive Advantage." *Journal of Management* 17 (1991): 99–121.

Barrett, J., and M. N. Rizza. "Supplier Collaboration: Are You Deriving Value from the Relationship?" *Supply Chain Management Review* (2009): 8–9.

Berry, Leonard L. "Cultivating Service Brand Equity." *Journal of Academy of Marketing Science* 28 (2000): 128–37.

Birkinshaw, Julian, and Neil Hood. "Characteristics of Foreign Subsidiaries in Industry Clusters." *Journal of International Business Studies* 31 (2000): 141–54.

Bitner, Mary Joe. "Building Service Relationships: It's All About Promises." *Journal of the Academy of Marketing Sciences* 23 (1995): 246–51.

Blumenberg, Stefan, Heinz-Theo Wagner, and Daniel Beimborn. "Knowledge Transfer Processes in IT Outsourcing Relationships and Their Impact on Shared Knowledge and Outsourcing Performance." *International Journal of Information Management* 29 (2009): 342–52.

Bustinza, O. F., L. M. Molina, and L. J. Gutierrez-Gutierrez. "Outsourcing As Seen from the Perspective of Knowledge Management." *Journal of Supply Chain Management* 46 (2010): 23–39.

Brodie, Roderick J., Mark S. Glynn, and Victoria Little. "The Service Brand and the Service-dominant Logic: Missing Fundamental Premise or the Need for Stronger Theory?" *Marketing Theory* 6 (2006): 363–76.

Chesbrough, Henry, and Richard S. Rosenbloom. "The Role of the Business Model in Capturing Value from Innovation: Evidence from Xerox Corporation's Technology Spinoff Companies." *Industrial and Corporate Change* 11, 533–534, 2002.

Clemons, Eric K., and Lorin M. Hitt. "Strategic Sourcing for Services: Assessing the Balance between Outsourcing and Insourcing." Working paper, 1997.

Cooper, C. Martha, Douglas M. Lambert, and Janus D. Pagh. "Supply Chain Management: More Than a New Name for Logistics." *International Journal of Logistics Management* 8 (1997): 1–14.

Cova, Bernard, and Robert Salle. "Marketing Solutions in Accordance with the S-D Logic: Co-creating Value with Customer Network Actors." *Industrial Marketing Management* 37 (2008): 270–7.

Danneels, Erwin. "The Dynamics of Product Innovation and Firm Competences." *Strategic Management Journal* 23 (2002): 1095–121.

Day, George S. "The Capabilities of Market-driven Organizations." *Journal of Marketing* 58 (1994): 37.

de Waart, Dirk, and Steve Kemper. "Five Steps to Service Supply Chain Excellence." *Supply Chain Management Review* 1 (2004): 30–5.

DeWitt, T., Giunipero L. C., and Melton H. L., Clusters and supply chain management: the Amish experience. *International Journal of Physical Sciences* 35 (2006): 289–308.

Edvardsson, B., M. Holmlund, and T. Strandvik. "Initiation of Business Relationships in Service-dominant Settings." *Industrial Marketing Management* 37 (2008): 339–50.

Ellram Lisa M., Wendy L. Tate, and Corey C. Billington. "Understanding and Managing the Service Supply chain." *Journal of Supply Chain Management* 40 (2004): 17–32.

Eisenmann, Thomas R. *Internet Business Models.* New York: McGraw-Hill Irwin, 2002.

Fisher, Marshall. "What is the Right Supply Chain for your Product?" *Harvard Business Review* (1997): 105–16.

Flint, Daniel J., and John T. Mentzer. "Striving for Integrated Value Chain Management: Given a Services Dominant Logic for Marketing," in *Toward a Service-Dominant Logic of Marketing: Dialogue, Debate, and Directions*, Eds. Robert F. Lusch and Stephen Vargo, M. E. Sharpe, Inc., 2006: 139–49.

Freeman, Edward R. *Strategic Management: A Stakeholder Approach*. Boston: Pitman, 1984.

Friedman, Thomas. *The World Is Flat: A Brief History of the Twenty-first Century.* Farrar, Straus and Giroux, 2005.

Fung, Victor K., William K. Fung, and Yoram (Jerry) Wind. *Competing in a Flat World.* Upper Saddle River, NJ: Wharton School Publishing, 2008.

Greenfield, Harry I. *Manpower and the Growth of Producer Services.* New York: Columbia University Press, 1966.

Gulati Ranjay. "Network Location and Learning: The Influence of Network Resources and Firm Capabilities on Alliance Formation." *Strategy Management Journal* 20 (1999): 397–420.

Grönroos, Christian. *Service Management and Marketing: A Customer Relationship Management Approach.* West Sussex, UK: John Wiley & Sons, 2000.

Hakansson, Hakan. *International Marketing and Purchasing of Industrial Goods: An Interaction Approach.* London: Wiley, 1982.

Hansen, Niles. "The Strategic Role of Producer Services in Regional Development." *International Regional Science Review* 16 (1994): 187,195.

Harrison, Bennett. "Industrial Districts: Old Wine in New Bottles?" *Regional Studies* 26 (1992): 469–83.

Hsu, Ling-Ling. "SCM System Effects on Performance for Interaction between Suppliers and Buyers. *Industrial Management and Data Systems* 105 (2005): 857–75.

Hunt, Shelby D., and Robert M. Morgan. "The Resource-advantage Theory of Competition: A Review." *Review of Marketing Research* 1 (2004): 153–205.

Jackson, R. W., and P. D. Cooper. "Unique Aspects of Marketing Industrial Services." *Industrial Marketing Management* 17 (1988): 111–8.

Juleff-Tranter, L. E. (1996). "Advanced Producer Services: Just a Service to Manufacturing?" *The Service Industries Journal*, 16 (1996), no. 3, 389–400.

Jüttner, Uta, Helen Peck, and Martin Christopher. "Supply Chain Risk Management: Outlining an Agenda for Future Research." *International Journal of Logistics: Research and Applications* 6 (2003): 197–210.

Lambert, Douglas M., Martha C. Cooper, and Janus D. Pagh. "Supply Chain Management: Implementation Issues and Research Opportunities." *The International Journal of Logistics Management* 9 (1998): 1–19.

Lambert, Douglas M., and Martha C. Cooper. "Issues in Supply Chain Management." *Industrial Marketing Management* 29 (2000): 65–83.

Lee, Hau L., and Corey Billington. "The Evolution of Supply-Chain-Management Models and Practice at Hewlett-Packard," *Interfaces* 25 (1995): 42–64.

Levinthal, Daniel A. and Mark Fichman. "Dynamics of Interorganizational Attachments: Auditor-client Relationships." *Administrative Science Quarterly* 33 (1998): 345–69.

Lwein, Y. Arie, Carmen B. Weigelt, and James D. Emery. "Adaptation and Selection in Strategy and Change: Perspectives on Strategic Change in Organizations," in *Handbook of Organizational Change and Development*, Ed. Poole, S. M., New York: Oxford University Press, 2003.

Li, M., and Choi T. Y. "Triads in Services Outsourcing: Bridge, Bridge Decay and Bridge Transfer." *Journal of Supply Chain Management* 45 (2009): 27–39.

Little, V. J. "Understanding Customer Value: An Action-Research Based Study of Contemporary Marketing Practice." Unpublished PhD thesis, University of Auckland, 2004.

Lovelock, Christopher H. "Classifying Services to Gain Strategic Marketing Insights." *Journal of Marketing* 47 (1983): 9–20.

Magretta, Joan. "Why Business Models Matter." *Harvard Business Review* 80 (5) (2002): 86, 92.

Millar, V. "Outsourcing Trends." Proceedings of the Outsourcing, Co-sourcing and In-sourcing Conference, University of California, Berkeley, 1994.

Mitchell, R. K., B. R. Agle, and D. J. Woo., "Toward a Theory of Stakeholder Identification and Salience: Defining the Principle of Who and What Really Counts." *Academy of Management Review* 22 (1997): 853–86.

Mitchell, D., and C. Coles. "The Ultimate Competitive Advantage of Continuing Business Model Innovation." *Journal of Business Strategy* 24, 15–21, 2003.

Morgan, Robert M., and Shelby D. Hunt. "The Comparative Advantage Theory of Competition." *Journal of Marketing* 59 (1995): 1–15.

Siggelkow, Nicolaj. "Change in the Presence of Fit: The Rise, Fall, and the Renaissance of Liz Clairborne." *Academy of Management Journal* 44, 838–857 (2001).

Oliver, C. "The Influence of Institutional and Task Environment Relationship on Organizational Performance: The Canadian Construction Industry." *Journal of Management Studies* 34 (1997): 99–124.

Peng, M. W. *Global Strategy*, trans. Liu Yi el. Renmin University Press, 2009.

Penrose, E. T. *The Theory of the Growth of the Firm*. New York: Wiley, 1959.

Porter, M. E. "Clusters and the New Economics of Competition." *Harvard Business Review* 74 (1998): 6–15; 77–91.

Ramani, G., and V. Kumar. "Interaction Orientation and Firm Performance." *Journal of Marketing* 72 (2008): 27–45.

Robert B., Handfield, Ernest L. Nichols. *Introduction to Supply Chain Management.* New Jersey: Prentice-Hall, 1999.

Saccani, N., P. Johansson P., and M. Perona. "Configuring the After-Sales Service Supply Chain: A Multiple Case Study," *International Journal of Production Economics*, 2007.

Schniederjans, M. J., A. M. Schniederjans, and D. G. Schniederjans. *Outsourcing and Insourcing in an International Context.* New York: M. E. Sharpe 2005.

Scott, J. T. "Purposive Diversification as a Motive for Merger." *International Journal of Industrial Organization* 7 (1989): 35–47.

Scott, R. W. "Institutions and Organization." Thousand Oaks, CA: Sage, 2001.

Sengupta, Kaushik, Daniel R. Heiser, and Lori S. Cook. "Manufacturing and Service Supply Chain Performance: A Comparative Analysis." *Journal of Supply Chain Management*, 2006.

Shamsie, J. The Context of Dominance: An Industry-Driven Framework for Exploiting Reputation." *Strategic Management Journal* 24 (2003): 199–215.

Shostack, G. Lynn. "Designing Services That Deliver." *Harvard Business Review* (1984): 133–9.

Song Hua, Chatterjee, S. R., and Jingliang C., "Achieving Competitive Advantage in Service Supply Chain: Evidence from the Chinese steel industry." *Chinese Management Studies* 5 (2011): 68–81.

Sturgeon, T., and R. Florida (2004). "Globalization, Deverticalization, and Employment in the Motor Vehicle Industry," in *Locating Global Advantage: Industry Dynamics in a Globalizing Economy*, Eds. M. Kenny and R. Florida, Palo Alto, CA: Stanford University Press, 2004.

Suchman, M. C. "Managing Legitimacy: Strategic and Institutional Approaches." *Academy of Management Review* 20 (1995), 571–610.

Tambunan, T., Promoting Small and Medium Enterprises with a Clustering Approach: A Policy Experience from Indonesia, *Journal of Small Business Management* 43 (2005): 138–54.

Teece, David J. "Explicating Dynamic Capabilities: The Nature and Microfoundations of (sustainable) Enterprise Performance." *Strategic Management Journal* 28 (2007): 1319–50.

Tuncdan, Baltacioglu, Erhan Ada, Melike Kaplan, Oznur Yurt, and Cem Kaplan Y. "A New Framework for Service Supply Chains." *The Services Industries Journal* 27 (2007): 105–24.

Vandermerwe, Sandra, and Juan Rada. "Servitization of Business: Adding Value by Adding Services." *European Management Journal* 6 (1988).

Van der Valk, Wendy, and Frank Rozemeijer. "Buying Business Services: Towards a Structured Service Purchasing Process." *Journal of Services Marketing* 23 (2009): 3–10.

Vargo, S. L., and Lusch R. F. "Evolving to a New Dominant Logic for Marketing." *Journal of Marketing* 68 (2004): 1–17.

Vargo, S. L. and Lusch R. F. "From Goods to Services: Divergence and Convergences of Logics. *Industrial Marketing Management* 37 (2008), 254–9.

Vitasek, K., and Ledyard M. "Vested Outsourcing: A Better Way to Outsource." *Supply Chain Management Review* (2009): 20–27.

Vitasek, K., and Ledyard M. "Changing the Game: Going the Whole Nine yards with Your Outsourcing Relationship." *Globalization Today* (2010): 31–9.

Youngdahl, William E., and Arvinder P. S. Loomba. "Service-driven Global Supply Chains." *International Journal of Service Industry Management*, 2000.

Zeithaml, V. A. "Consumer Perception of Price, Quality, and Value: A Means-End Model and Synthesis of Evidence." *Journal of Marketing* 52 (1988): 2–22.

Ulaga W. Capturing Value Creation in Business Relationships: A Customer Perspective." *Industrial Marketing Management* 32 (2003): 677–93.

Wernerfelt, B. "Reputation, Monitoring, and Effort." *Information Economics and Policy* 3 (1988): 207–18.

Willcocks, L., and M. C. Lacity. *Strategic Sourcing of Information Systems*. Chichester: Wiley, 1998.

Williamson, O. E., "The Theory of the Firm as Governance Structure: From Choice to Contract." *Journal of Economic Perspectives* 16 (2002): 171–95.

Woodruff, R. B. "Customer Value: The Next Source for Competitive Advantage." *Journal of the Academy of Marketing Science* 25 (1997): 139–53.

Wynstra, F., B. Axelsson, and W. Van der Valk. "An Application-based Classification to Understand Buyer–supplier Interaction in Business Services." *International Journal of Service Industry Management* 17 (2006): 474–96.

Zaheer, A., and Venkatraman N. "Relational Governance as an Interorganizational Strategy: An Empirical Test of the Role of Trust in Economic Exchange. *Strategy Management Journal* 16 (1995): 373–92.

Zeithaml, Valarie A., and Mary Jo Bitner. *Services Marketing*. McGraw-Hill Companies, 1996.

Index